MASTERS OF ART

LEONARDO DA VINCI

Artist, inventor and scientist of the Renaissance

FRANCESCA ROMEI

◆

ILLUSTRATED BY
SERGIO, ANDREA RICCIARDI

SIMON & SCHUSTER

DoGi

Produced by
Donati-Giudici Associati, Florence
Text
Francesca Romei
Illustrations
Sergio
Andrea Ricciardi
Editorial coordination
Francesco Fiorentino
Art direction and design
Oliviero Ciriaci
Research
Francesca Donati
Editing
Enza Fontana
Pagination
Monica Macchiaioli
Desktop publishing
Ugo Micheli
English translation
Simon Knight
Editor, English-language edition
Ruth Nason
Typesetting
Ken Alston – A.J. Latham Ltd.

© 1994 Donati-Giudici Associati s.r.l.
English language text © 1994 by
Simon & Schuster Young
Books/Peter Bedrick Books
First published in Great Britain
in 1994 by
Simon & Schuster Young Books
Campus 400
Maylands Avenue
Hemel Hempstead
Herts HP2 7EZ

ISBN 0 7500 1609 4

Printed in Italy
by Amilcare Pizzi S.p.A.

◆ How the information is presented

ILLUSTRATED PAGES

Every double-page spread is devoted to a particular theme. The main illustration is a faithful reconstruction of a given environment, or represents a significant incident or event.

The text at the top of the left-hand page interprets this illustration. The text in italics gives a chronological account of developments in Leonardo's life. The other material (photographs, paintings, drawings, artefacts) enlarges on the central theme.

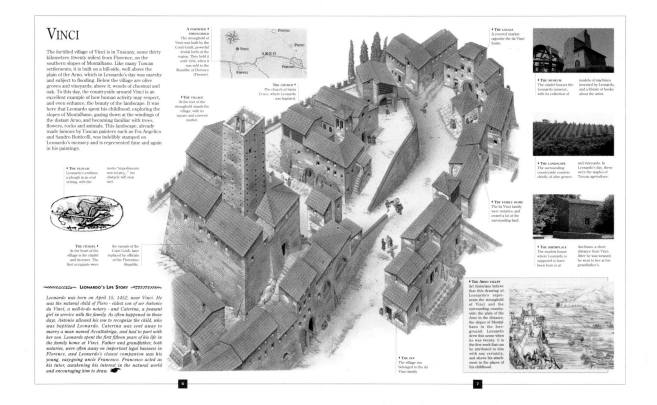

PAGES DEVOTED TO WORKS OF ART

Some pages focus on the great works of art created by Leonardo. They include background information about the painting, in the left-hand column; a description of the work, at the top; a detailed

analysis of certain aspects of the work; an explanation of its significance and the technical problems involved, in italics; and comparisons with works by other artists, which highlight the historical context and the originality of Leonardo's approach to the subject.

CONTENTS

CONTEMPORARIES

Born in Tuscany in the mid-fifteenth century, Leonardo da Vinci excelled in painting, sculpture, music, mathematics, engineering and architecture. In the wealthy and cultured city of Florence he was apprenticed to one of the outstanding artists of the time, Andrea del Verrocchio. During his life he came into contact with some of the key figures of European politics: Lorenzo the Magnificent, ruler of Florence; Ludovico il Moro, lord of Milan; the Pope; and two kings of France. Of the artists and scientists of the Renaissance, Leonardo was the one who best summed up the new culture. He represents a new understanding of the world, and of man's capacity to penetrate the mysteries of nature and the human mind.

♦ FILIPPO BRUNELLESCHI ♦
(1377-1446)
The greatest Florentine architect of the Renaissance.

♦ MASACCIO ♦
(1401-1428)
Tuscan painter, the first artist to use perspective systematically.

♦ LEONARDO'S FATHER AND MOTHER
His father, ser Piero di Antonio, was a well-known notary; his mother, Caterina, a peasant girl in service with the family.

SANDRO BOTTICELLI ♦
(1445-1510)
Florentine painter. Like Leonardo, he trained in Verrocchio's workshop.

MICHELANGELO ♦ BUONARROTI
(1475-1564)
Sculptor, painter, architect and poet. A great Italian artist.

DONATO BRAMANTE ♦
(1444-1514)
Architect and painter. With Leonardo, he served Ludovico il Moro, lord of Milan.

♦ LEONARDO
Often portrayed with a long beard, Leonardo was described by his contemporaries as outstandingly good-looking.

♦ ANDREA DEL VERROCCHIO (1435-1488) Goldsmith, sculptor and painter. Leonardo was trained in his workshop.

♦ LUCA PACIOLI
(1445-1514)
Franciscan friar and man of science. He knew Leonardo in Milan, and awakened his interest in mathematics.

♦ ZOROASTRO
Skilled in mechanics, and metal work, he made models for Leonardo's designs.

FRANCESCO MELZI ♦
(1493-1570)
Leonardo's favourite pupil. He followed his master to France and, on his death, inherited his manuscripts and paintings.

♦ NICCOLÒ MACHIAVELLI
Writer, philosopher and political theorist. He was secretary to the Florentine Republic after the fall of the Medicis.

♦ PIERO SODERINI
Head of the Florentine Republic. He commissioned important works from Leonardo.

♦ ISABELLA D'ESTE
Marchioness of Mantua. Leonardo drew her portrait in 1499.

♦ LOUIS XII
King of France from 1498 to 1515. He conquered Lombardy in 1499 and commissioned several works of art from Leonardo.

♦ RAFFAELLO SANZIO (RAPHAEL) (1483-1520)
Painter and architect. With Leonardo and Michelangelo, he is considered the greatest Italian artist of the period.

♦ LUDOVICO IL MORO
Ruler of Milan. In 1482 he invited Leonardo to live at his court.

♦ CECILIA GALLERANI
Ludovico il Moro's mistress and a key figure at the Sforza court. She protected Leonardo, and he painted a famous portrait of her.

CHARLES OF AMBOISE ♦
Governor of Milan in the early years of the sixteenth century. Leonardo planned a palace for him in Milan, but it was never built.

♦ LORENZO THE MAGNIFICENT
Head of the Medici family. He ruled the city of Florence during a period of great cultural and artistic brilliance.

♦ FRANCIS I
He succeeded Louis XII as king of France. In 1517 he invited Leonardo to France, and gave him a splendid manor house to live in.

VINCI

The fortified village of Vinci is in Tuscany, some thirty kilometres (twenty miles) from Florence, on the southern slopes of Montalbano. Like many Tuscan settlements, it is built on a hill-side, well above the plain of the Arno, which in Leonardo's day was marshy and subject to flooding. Below the village are olive groves and vineyards; above it, woods of chestnut and oak. To this day, the countryside around Vinci is an excellent example of how human activity may respect, and even enhance, the beauty of the landscape. It was here that Leonardo spent his childhood: exploring the slopes of Montalbano, gazing down at the windings of the distant Arno, and becoming familiar with trees, flowers, rocks and animals. This landscape, already made famous by Tuscan painters such as Fra Angelico and Sandro Botticelli, was indelibly stamped on Leonardo's memory and is represented time and again in his paintings.

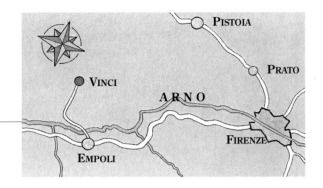

A FORTIFIED ✦ STRONGHOLD
The stronghold of Vinci was built by the Conti Guidi, powerful feudal lords of the region. They held it until 1254, when it was sold to the Republic of Florence (Firenze).

✦ THE VILLAGE
At the foot of the stronghold stands the village, with its square and covered market.

THE CHURCH ✦
The church of Santa Croce, where Leonardo was baptized.

✦ THE PLOUGH
Leonardo's emblem: a plough in an oval setting, with the motto "impedimento non mi piega" (no obstacle will stop me).

THE CITADEL ✦
At the heart of the village is the citadel and its tower. The first occupants were the vassals of the Conti Guidi, later replaced by officials of the Florentine Republic.

∿∿∿∿∿✦ LEONARDO'S LIFE STORY ✦∿∿∿∿∿

Leonardo was born on April 15, 1452, near Vinci. He was the natural child of Piero - eldest son of ser Antonio da Vinci, a well-to-do notary - and Caterina, a peasant girl in service with the family. As often happened in those days, Antonio allowed his son to recognize the child, who was baptized Leonardo. Caterina was sent away to marry a man named Accattabriga, and had to part with her son. Leonardo spent the first fifteen years of his life in the family home at Vinci. Father and grandfather, both notaries, were often away on important legal business in Florence, and Leonardo's closest companion was his young, easy-going uncle Francesco. Francesco acted as his tutor, awakening his interest in the natural world and encouraging him to draw. ☞

✦ THE LOGGIA
A covered market near the da Vinci home.

✦ THE MUSEUM
The citadel houses the Leonardo museum, with its collection of models of machines invented by Leonardo, and a library of books about the artist.

✦ THE LANDSCAPE
The surrounding countryside consists chiefly of olive groves and vineyards. In Leonardo's day, these were the staples of Tuscan agriculture.

✦ THE FAMILY HOME
The da Vinci family were notaries, and owned a lot of the surrounding land.

✦ THE BIRTHPLACE
The modest house where Leonardo is supposed to have been born is at Anchiano, a short distance from Vinci. After he was weaned, he went to live at his grandfather's.

✦ THE ARNO VALLEY
Art historians believe that this drawing of Leonardo's represents the stronghold of Vinci and the surrounding countryside: the plain of the Arno in the distance, the slopes of Montalbano in the foreground. Leonardo drew this scene when he was twenty. It is the first work that can be attributed to him with any certainty, and shows his attachment to the places of his childhood.

✦ THE INN
The village inn belonged to the da Vinci family.

FLORENCE

Florence, as Leonardo first experienced it in 1467, was one of the major centres of European culture. Although the Black Death, in the middle of the fourteenth century, had halved the city's population and arrested its growth, Florence had reacted energetically to become one of the world's main places of business and trade. During the fifteenth century, the city enjoyed a long spell of political stability, which led to an extraordinary flowering of the arts. Florence was the cradle of Humanism and the Renaissance. By the time Leonardo arrived on the scene, the first fruits of this revolution were clearly visible. The great families, led by the Medicis, had abandoned their austere medieval houses in favour of elegant new residences. They built churches, convents and hospitals, and enriched the city with works of art. To complete their cathedral, the Florentines commissioned a dome of extraordinary daring. Florence was not governed by tyrants like many of its neighbours. The patronage which transformed the face of the city was dispensed by a ruling class of bankers and merchants.

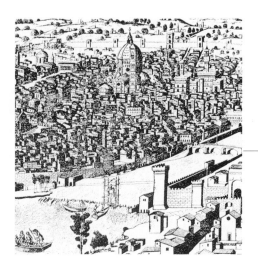

✦ THE CITY
This view of Florence, drawn some time between 1471 and 1482, helps us to reconstruct the city as it would have looked in Leonardo's day.

☞ *In 1467 Piero da Vinci's career dictated that he settle in Florence and marry a woman of his own social class. Leonardo accompanied him. With his father and young stepmother, he lived in a house near the Piazza della Signoria. Piero served the government as a notary, took part in politics, and turned his attention to his son's education. Leonardo had lessons in music, grammar and geometry. He was a ready pupil, with a curious, restless temperament. The story goes that, having quickly mastered the abacus, an ancient instrument for making calculations, he confused his teacher with a string of searching questions. He was particularly gifted in music and excelled in playing the lyre. The new interests did not dampen his enthusiasm for drawing, which remained his dominant passion.* ☞

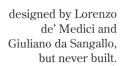

A PROJECT ✦ NEVER FULFILLED
Ground plan of a grandiose palace designed by Lorenzo de' Medici and Giuliano da Sangallo, but never built.

SANTISSIMA ✦ ANNUNZIATA
A church built by Michelozzo from 1444. The raised loggia (1447) was designed by Alberti.

OSPEDALE DEGLI ✦ INNOCENTI
A hospital built by Filippo Brunelleschi in 1419 to care for abandoned children.

CONVENT OF ✦ SAN MARCO
Built by Michelozzo in 1436-44 for Cosimo il Vecchio. In 1438-46 Fra Angelico adorned the cells, cloister and chapter room with fresco paintings.

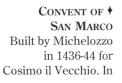

PALAZZO MEDICI ✦
Cosimo il Vecchio commissioned the Medici residence, which was built by Michelozzo, 1444-59.

SAN LORENZO ✦
One of Florence's oldest churches, remodelled for the Medicis by Brunelleschi in 1442.

PALAZZO STROZZI ✦
Building of this residence for Palla Strozzi was begun by Benedetto da Maiano in 1489 and completed by Simone del Pollaiuolo, who designed the cornice and inner courtyard.

SANTA MARIA NOVELLA ✦
This church houses Masaccio's *Trinità*, 1427. The façade was built by Leon Battista Alberti in 1470.

PALAZZO RUCELLAI ✦
The palace was built in the years 1447 to 1451. Leon Battista Alberti designed the façade.

THE CITY WALLS ✦
Built between 1287 and 1321 to accommodate the city's growing population, which then numbered some 100,000 inhabitants.

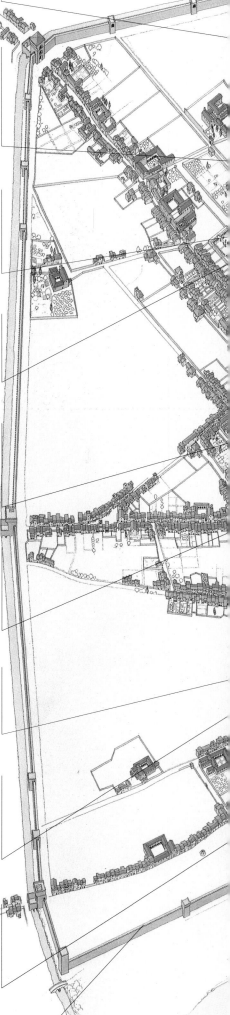

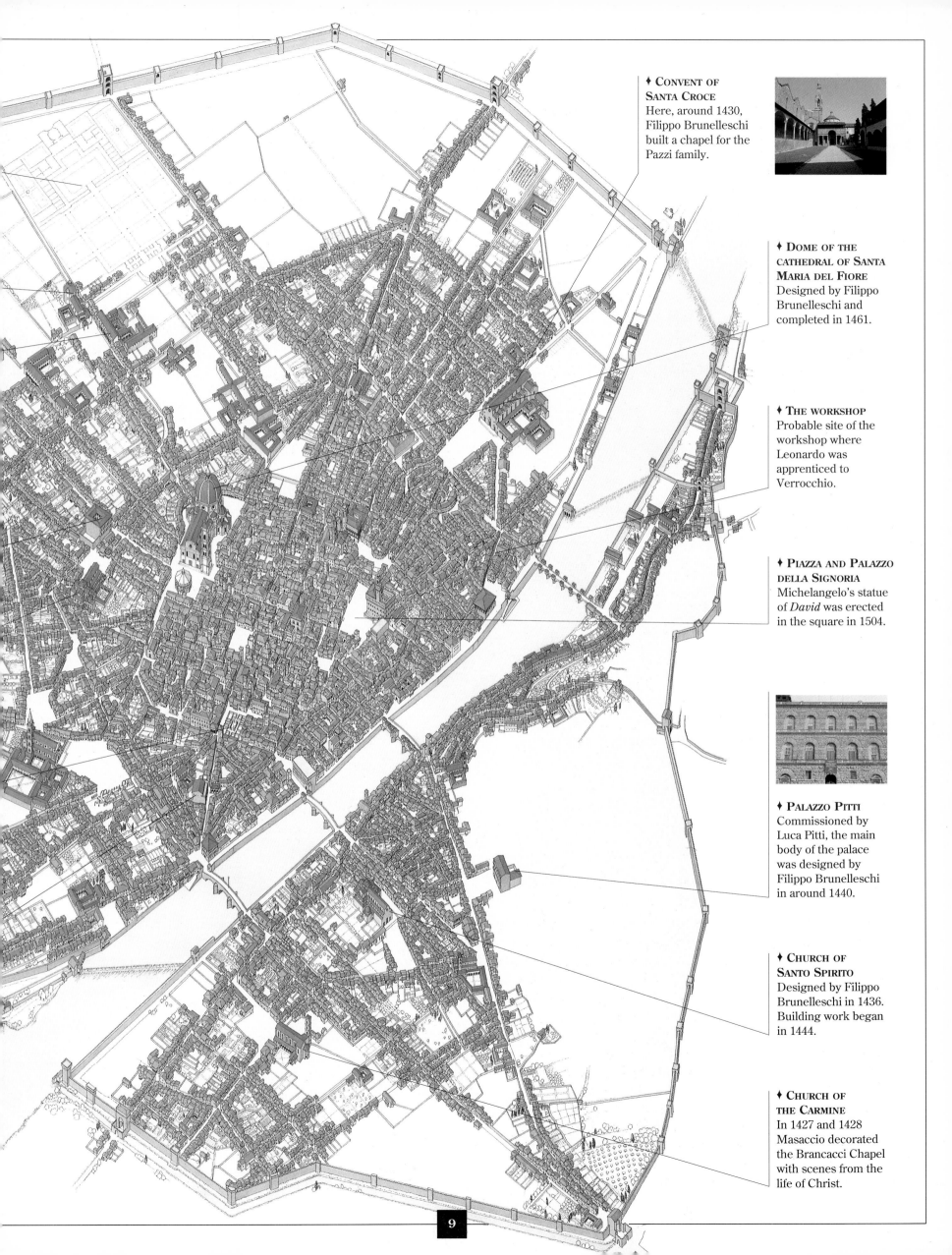

♦ **CONVENT OF SANTA CROCE**
Here, around 1430, Filippo Brunelleschi built a chapel for the Pazzi family.

♦ **DOME OF THE CATHEDRAL OF SANTA MARIA DEL FIORE**
Designed by Filippo Brunelleschi and completed in 1461.

♦ **THE WORKSHOP**
Probable site of the workshop where Leonardo was apprenticed to Verrocchio.

♦ **PIAZZA AND PALAZZO DELLA SIGNORIA**
Michelangelo's statue of *David* was erected in the square in 1504.

♦ **PALAZZO PITTI**
Commissioned by Luca Pitti, the main body of the palace was designed by Filippo Brunelleschi in around 1440.

♦ **CHURCH OF SANTO SPIRITO**
Designed by Filippo Brunelleschi in 1436. Building work began in 1444.

♦ **CHURCH OF THE CARMINE**
In 1427 and 1428 Masaccio decorated the Brancacci Chapel with scenes from the life of Christ.

THE RENAISSANCE

Renaissance means "new birth". The idea of a new beginning based on classical Greek and Roman art, and direct observation of the natural world, was embraced by many fifteenth-century artists and men of letters. The civilization born in Florence and the prosperous Low Countries (Flanders) in the early years of the fifteenth century was to influence all areas of human activity: the organization of society, economics, art and science. The main features of Renaissance painting and sculpture are a desire to investigate and represent the real world - evident in the works of great Tuscan artists such as Masaccio and Donatello, or Flemish masters like Van Eyck - and a systematic study of Greek and Roman models. In architecture, whose greatest exponent was Filippo Brunelleschi, we find a new reliance on reason, which made it possible to solve complex problems of building technique. In philosophy and science, for the first time in history, humankind came to be regarded as the centre of the universe

♦TWO CRUCIFIXES
Sometime between 1410 and 1415, Brunelleschi carved a wooden crucifix for the church of Santa Maria Novella (above). Christ is depicted with a composed expression and a body of classical perfection. The light caresses the polished surfaces, creating a soft, hazy effect and emphasizing the harmonious proportions. At around the same time, Donatello also carved a crucifix, which can be seen in the church of Santa Croce. His is a tortured Christ, face pinched and body racked with pain. In this case, the natural lighting heightens the intensity of the figure, striking the awkwardly angled planes and creating violent contrasts of light and shade. Donatello was harshly criticized for having "crucified a peasant".

BRUNELLESCHI ♦
In 1430 Filippo Brunelleschi built the Pazzi Chapel in the cloister of Santa Croce, Florence. It is considered one of his masterpieces.

ALBERTI ♦
In 1452 Leon Battista Alberti wrote a treatise on architecture. Though not published until a century later, it had an enormous influence on the new Renaissance style of building.

PAOLO UCCELLO ♦
Between 1456 and 1460 the Florentine artist Paolo Uccello painted three large canvases on the subject of the victory of Florence over Siena in the battle of San Romano in 1432.

♦NANNI DI BANCO
Four Crowned Saints, for the Florentine church of Orsanmichele. With Brunelleschi and Ghiberti, Nanni di Banco is one of the pioneering figures in Renaissance sculpture.

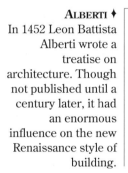

♦THE SACRIFICE OF ISAAC
In 1401 a competition was held for relief sculptures to adorn one of the doors of the baptistry in Florence. Among the candidates were the young sculptors Lorenzo Ghiberti and Filippo Brunelleschi. Brunelleschi's trial panel (below left) was considered too revolutionary: he had arranged his figures freely, with parts projecting outside the confines of the frame. Ghiberti, whose entry is shown above, was more traditional and ordered in his approach. It was he who won the commission.

☞ *In Florence, the workshops of goldsmiths, painters and sculptors were on every street. The churches were adorned with major works of art, and it was not unusual to come across an artist intent on a new commission. Leonardo was a young man of insatiable curiosity: he would visit the craftsmen's workshops, and enthuse over the new works of art he saw being created. He also took an interest in the machinery and tools used by architects and artists. On visits to the surrounding countryside and gardens, he made drawings of plants, birds and insects to improve his powers of observation. His father, meanwhile, pursued a successful career in law, and would have liked Leonardo to follow in his footsteps. But Leonardo was beginning to show signs of strong leanings in a quite different direction.* ☞

MASACCIO ♦

In 1427 and 1428 Masaccio decorated the Brancacci Chapel in the Florentine church of the Carmine. In his fresco of the *Tribute Money*, he used perspective and the interplay of light and shade to create a new, more realistic sense of space. The window of the chapel is to the right of his mural, and Masaccio painted the scene as if the light were falling from the same direction. The picture, therefore, appears to be a continuation of the real environment.

♦ FACES

In the intensity of facial expression depicted by Masaccio, we sense moral depth and a heroic view of human destiny. His characters belong to a human-centred universe.

DONATELLO ♦

Feast of Herod, executed in 1427 for the baptismal font of San Giovanni in Siena. The bronze panel combines a "schiacciato", or "flattened", low-relief technique with the use of scientific linear perspective, to give a sense of depth.

♦ HUGO VAN DER GOES

A triptych painted by Hugo van der Goes for the Florentine banker Tommaso Portinari arrived in Florence in 1483, and was displayed in the church of Sant'Egidio. These flowers are from the foreground of the central panel of the triptych which represents the *Adoration of the Shepherds*. The Flemish painters showed great interest in the natural world and paid minute attention to detail.

♦ VAN EYCK

Giovanni Arnolfini and his wife was executed in 1434 by the Flemish painter Jan van Eyck (1390-1441). His work was much admired in Italy, where his use of perspective gave further impetus to the revolution begun by Masaccio. It used to be said that Van Eyck invented oil paint, which enabled him to achieve novel effects in depicting light and atmosphere.

PERSPECTIVE

Linear perspective was the great innovation of Renaissance painting. Using precise mathematical principles, artists discovered how to represent a three-dimensional view as perceived in reality, even though they were working on a flat, two-dimensional surface. Objects and figures were positioned in the picture space, so that it seemed to recede towards a single central vanishing point. At the unveiling of Masaccio's fresco of the *Trinity* in the Florentine church of Santa Maria Novella, the on-lookers could hardly believe their eyes: it was as if the painter had really carved out a chapel in the wall and placed his figures at different distances, such was the illusion of space he had created. The inventor of perspective may well have been Brunelleschi, but it was Leon Battista Alberti who first dealt with the subject systematically, in a treatise he wrote in 1435. Another artist, Piero della Francesca, developed the technique further, publishing a treatise on the subject in 1478. Leonardo later wrote a contribution of his own, but the manuscript has been lost.

MASACCIO'S GENIUS ✦
In 1427 Masaccio painted a fresco of the *Trinity* for the church of Santa Maria Novella, using a perspective technique developed by Brunelleschi. In the setting of a chapel, he depicted Christ Crucified, with God the Father and the dove of the Holy Spirit behind, and St John and the Virgin Mary on either side. Mary points to Christ, while looking out of the picture space towards the observer. Outside, Masaccio depicted the donors, who appear to be worshipping in the body of the church. The *Trinity* was a new departure in Florentine painting. Unlike their medieval counterparts, who did not attempt to portray religious subjects in a real setting, Renaissance artists sought to create the illusion of space and depth. The faithful could then feel involved in the scenes before them.

PERSPECTIVE ✦ PAINTED
The illusion of depth is evident in this detail from Piero della Francesca's painting of the *Annunciation*. By foreshortening the columns, he has given the church a sense of space and volume.

AND IN REALITY ✦
Photograph of a side aisle, church of Santo Spirito, Florence. Comparison with the painted scene on the left reveals strong similarities. Painters often practised perspective techniques by drawing architectural features.

✦ THE MEDIEVAL VIEW
In the Middle Ages painters did sometimes make use of perspective, but their methods were unscientific. Their approach gave them the freedom to represent the various stages of a story in one and the same picture, or to depict people and things large or small, according to their importance. In his fresco of *St Francis expelling the devils from Arezzo*, Giotto shows us the inside and outside of the town, devils bigger than houses, and the saint almost as tall as the apse of the basilica on his left.

A PERSPECTOGRAPH ♦
The painter observes a globe from a fixed point and draws its outline on a transparent screen. Instruments like this perspectograph were much used by Renaissance artists.

♦ **THE ILLUSION OF PERSPECTIVE**
To enjoy the perspective effect to the full, the observer must stand at a certain distance from Masaccio's fresco.

This then gives the impression of looking into a real chapel, with the figures arranged - some inside, some outside - as shown in this diagram.

♦ **THE RENAISSANCE ARTISTS' VIEW**
Renaissance artists represented three-dimensional space as it is perceived in reality. In this painting of the *Baptism of Christ*, by Piero della Francesca (c. 1410/20-92), all lines converge on the central figure. The landscape behind him has been precisely constructed to create an illusion of depth, with objects apparently receding into the distance. All parts of the painting have a geometrical simplicity and are shown smaller, the further they are from the scene in the foreground.

☞ Ser Piero da Vinci, who had meanwhile been appointed to the prestigious post of procurator to the convent of the Santissima Annunziata, finally had to admit defeat: his son was not cut out to be a lawyer. His artistic leanings were too strong. The vocation that had been stirred to life during Leonardo's care-free early years in the countryside around Vinci blossomed in the first period he spent in Florence. There, in the church of Santa Croce, he admired the frescoes Giotto had painted just over a century before; at Santa Maria Novella and in the church of the Carmine, he could wonder at Masaccio's murals, only a few decades old. There were great opportunities for a young man aspiring to be an artist. Antonio del Pollaiuolo, a famous sculptor and painter, and Andrea del Cione, nicknamed Verrocchio, were the leading masters of the day, and an apprenticeship in their workshops was highly sought after. Ser Piero was attracted by the reputation of Verrocchio's workshop, where, it was said, there was opportunity to master many different techniques and be involved in important commissions. ☞

VERROCCHIO'S WORKSHOP

Traditionally, artists' workshops in fifteenth-century Florence produced a wide range of artefacts: paintings of religious and secular subjects, sculptures in terracotta, marble and bronze, decorated objects for use in the home, gold and silverware, painted banners and coats of arms, death masks, and designs and prototypes of machinery for peaceful and military purposes. Andrea del Verrocchio was outstanding in all these activities, and his workshop attracted the most talented young men. Some of the greatest artists of the century trained with him: Pietro Vannucci, known as Perugino, Lorenzo di Credi and Sandro Botticelli, who served for some years as Verrocchio's assistant, after an initial period with the painter Filippo Lippi. Following a long-standing Florentine tradition, drawing was given special attention, with the emphasis on accuracy.

♦ DEATH MASKS
Verrocchio was highly skilled in taking impressions of the faces of dead people, using a mixture of plaster and warm water. His skill was much in demand. The white images were often copied in marble or cast in bronze.

♦ NUDE STUDY
A preparatory study by Verrocchio for an intended statue.

♦ THE COPPER BALL
As an engineer, Verrocchio had been commissioned to construct an enormous gilded copper ball to adorn the dome of the cathedral.

PIERO DA VINCI ♦ AND VERROCCHIO
Piero da Vinci showed Verrocchio drawings that Leonardo had been doing almost in secret. "Leave your son with me," Verrocchio is supposed to have said. "We'll make something of him."

♦ A YOUNG TEACHER
Born in 1435, Verrocchio was little more than thirty years old when Leonardo entered his workshop.

♦ A DRAPERY STUDY BY LEONARDO
So that pupils in the workshop could practise drawing drapery, a piece of fabric was arranged on an appropriate support, then impregnated with glue to fix the contours. Leonardo made this study in 1478.

♦ LORENZO DI CREDI
A portrait of the painter Perugino by his pupil, Lorenzo di Credi.

BOTTICELLI ♦
A drawing by Botticelli, who was also one of Verrocchio's pupils.

♦ MASTER AND PUPIL
This is a workshop study for a painting of *Venus and Cupid*. Verrocchio and his young apprentice Leonardo worked on it together.

♦ DRAWING
For figures and faces, live models were used; the folds of clothing, which required days of patient and painstaking work, were drawn from dummies.

♦ PAINTS
One of the first tasks of the apprentices: grinding pigments.

In 1469 Leonardo was apprenticed to Verrocchio, a famous goldsmith, sculptor, painter and engineer. His workshop consisted of several rooms. The main room was used for metal work, carving and modelling statues, and drawing; the others for preparing the materials needed for the various activities. Normally, an apprentice would enter the workshop at the age of twelve. He would begin by learning the humblest tasks: sweeping up, and grinding and mixing paints. Leonardo was already seventeen, and sufficiently mature to turn his hand to drawing. Under Verrocchio's guidance, he learned the techniques of line drawing and shading in silver point, how to make rapid ink sketches, the secrets of perspective, and how to bring a portrait to life.

PAINTING

At the time of Leonardo's apprenticeship, the main characteristic of Florentine painting was a concern for outline. Subtle, distinctly-drawn contours were used to make the figures stand out from the surrounding space, and emphasize anatomical details and the folds of clothing. But some painters - Domenico Veneziano and Piero della Francesca, in Florence, and particularly the artists of the powerful and magnificent city of Venice - were experimenting with different techniques. They based their compositions on the juxtaposition or contrast of colours. Michelangelo, who was about twenty years younger than Leonardo, summed up the situation with a characteristic touch of irony: "God is always even-handed: to the Florentines he gave drawing; to the Venetians, colour." From the very start of his career, when he was asked to help paint the *Baptism of Christ*, Leonardo adopted a highly individual way of blending his colours, to create a clear, limpid atmosphere.

BOTTICELLI'S USE ✦ OF OUTLINE
A detail from Sandro Botticelli's *Birth of Venus*, painted in 1482. The various areas of different colours are separated by clearly defined lines.

BELLINI'S USE ✦ OF COLOUR
In this *Pietà* by the Venetian Giovanni Bellini (1432-1516), the outlines of the figures are less distinct, their contours suggested by delicate gradations of colour.

✦ THE BAPTISM OF CHRIST
The work was painted between 1472 and 1475 for the cloister of the church of San Salvi, in Florence. Leonardo's contribution was the angel on the left and the landscape to the left of the standing Christ.

✦ UNDER VERROCCHIO'S WATCHFUL EYE
The apprentice at work. According to tradition, Leonardo's extraordinary ability was the cause of his master giving up painting.

LEFT-HANDED ✦
Leonardo was left-handed. Here, he puts the final touches to the angel's head, using a support to steady his hand.

☞ *As ser Piero had been informed, Verrocchio's workshop was asked to carry out important commissions. The* Baptism of Christ *is a good example. As was customary, the master's best pupils were also engaged on the work. Leonardo was given the task of executing the head of one of the angels, and the landscape behind them: a valley with a river running through it. According to legend, Leonardo painted the angel on the left so perfectly that Verrocchio decided to give up painting, breaking his paint-brush in a gesture of surrender before the superior skill of his young pupil. In fact, it was Verrocchio's training that led Leonardo to strive for formal perfection in his rendering of figures and landscapes. The perfect combination of subjects and natural setting is the hallmark of his later, mature works.* ☞

♦ **THE ANGEL**
Leonardo probably
only did the painting.
The figure would
have been drawn by
Verrocchio.

♦ **THE LANDSCAPE** ♦
The landscape of
rocks and running
water depicted by
Leonardo on this first
occasion was to
remain a constant
feature of his work.

♦ **TEMPERA**
In tempera painting
the pigments are
diluted with water
and egg yolk, and dry
very quickly. The
artist makes
corrections over the
original layer of paint.

♦ **OIL**
In oil painting the
pigments are diluted
with raw linseed oil.
The paint dries more
slowly, and the
composition can
therefore be
reworked over a
period of several
days.

♦ **MIXED TECHNIQUE**
At around this time,
oil painting was
introduced into Italy
by Flemish painters,
and the new
technique gradually
replaced the old
tradition of tempera
painting. The
transition is apparent
in Leonardo's
Annunciation: he
painted the angel and
the landscape in oils;
the rest of the
composition in
tempera.

THE ANNUNCIATION

The Archangel Gabriel, sent to Nazareth, greeted Joseph's intended bride with the words: "Do not be afraid, Mary, for God has been gracious to you: you shall conceive and bear a son, and you shall give him the name Jesus." This is St Luke's account of the Annunciation, and he adds that Mary drew back, deeply troubled. Leonardo's painting of this famous scene, for the monks of San Bartolomeo at Monteoliveto, was his first independent commission. He used a number of traditional symbols, as in earlier paintings of the subject: the lily in the angel's hand is a sign of purity and chastity; the grass and flowers typify spring-time; the book lying open on the lectern recalls Isaiah's prophecy that a virgin would conceive and bring forth a son.

♦ THE WORK
Oil and tempera on wooden panel, 98 x 217 cm (39 x 85 inches). Uffizi Gallery, Florence. The painting stayed at the monastery of San Bartolomeo until 1867, when it was transferred to the Uffizi Gallery. The marble sarcophagus

♦ BOTTICELLI
Botticelli, who worked on this *Annunciation* during the same period, around 1470, sets his figures in an open gallery, with a low wall cutting off the more distant view. The trees above the wall are reminiscent of those in Leonardo's painting.

was inspired by Verrocchio's decoration of Piero de' Medici's tomb in San Lorenzo, and the influence of another famous painter and sculptor of the period, Antonio del Pollaiuolo, can also be detected. This suggests a very early date for the work, between 1470 and 1471. Leonardo may even have completed this *Annunciation* before he painted the angel in Verrocchio's *Baptism of Christ*.

Having made a number of preparatory drawings to fix the positions and gestures of the figures, the details of the landscape and the architectural setting, Leonardo began to organize the surface of his panel. He sub-divided the picture space into several equal parts, creating a framework in which to arrange the various elements of the composition. As we study this Annunciation, *we become aware that*

Leonardo chose a very regular arrangement. The empty areas of landscape in the background alternate with the figures in the foreground, giving his work the rhythm and balance of a phrase of music. The hand of the angel raised in blessing corresponds to the Virgin's defensive gesture of surprise.

♦ ANOTHER ANNUNCIATION
Strong similarities between the panel in the Uffizi and the small *Annunciation* (below), now in the Louvre, suggest that the latter was also painted by Leonardo as a young man. It formed part of the predella for the *Madonna di Piazza*, a work commissioned from Verrocchio but actually painted by Lorenzo di Credi for the Cathedral in Pistoia.

THE VIRGIN ✦

Some errors show in Leonardo's perspective layout: one arm appears bigger than the other, and there is an awkwardness in the way the right arm rests on the lectern.

✦ SPILLING OUT OF THE PICTURE

The angel's garment is cut off by the left-hand edge of the picture, which seems to spill out of its frame. In this way, Leonardo created an illusion of continuity between the picture and its real setting.

FILIPPO LIPPI ✦

A Florentine painter active in the first half of the fifteenth century, Filippo Lippi worked on this *Annunciation* in the years 1437 to 1440 for the church of San Lorenzo, where it can still be seen. The architectural setting, with a foreshortened view of an internal courtyard in the background, shows an interest in perspective that is typical of Florentine painting of the period.

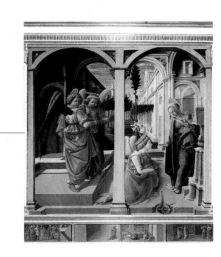

✦ A GEOMETRICAL COMPOSITION

Leonardo arranged his painting on geometrical lines. The straight lines of the wall and building give the design strength. The four pine trees, set at regular intervals serve to divide the picture space into equal rectangles; and the figures, which occupy their own triangular areas, create a series of five triangles across the picture.

✦ DOMENICO VENEZIANO

Domenico Veneziano was born in Venice and came to Florence around 1439. One of his assistants was Piero della Francesca. In this *Annunciation*, painted for the Florentine church of Santa Lucia dei Magnoli, the two slender figures in a simple setting emphasize the miraculous nature of the event.

MACHINES

Until quite recently it was thought that the many drawings of construction-site machinery contained in Leonardo's notebooks were purely the fruit of his teeming imagination: designs for futuristic devices unrelated to the technology of his own time. We now know that many of the machines he drew had in fact been built, particularly by Brunelleschi, and that Leonardo watched them at work on the cathedral building site in Florence. From the twelfth century, when Gothic architecture developed and flourished, cathedral building sites were the great centres of technical achievement, rather like modern-day satellite launch pads. On these sites, architects, carpenters, engineers, blacksmiths and mechanics from all over Europe met and exchanged knowledge and experience. They planned and built amazing machines, now long forgotten. We have Leonardo to thank for keeping a record of some of these machines. His drawings are so accurate that it has been possible to reconstruct them.

♦ THE DOME
Brunelleschi began building the cathedral dome in 1420. At his death, in 1446, only the lantern remained unfinished. Twenty-five years later Verrocchio's great copper sphere was fixed in place.

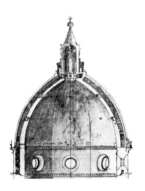

♦ A MASTERPIECE OF ENGINEERING
The dome was to be so huge, that Brunelleschi had to devise innovative internal scaffolding to support it. There are, in fact, an inner and an outer dome, making a double shell held together by the eight massive vertical ribs.

♦ "CONES"
Each layer of bricks is like part of a "cone". Because each layer is inclined towards a different point on the central axis, the "cones" fit together, each one into the next.

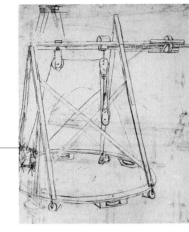

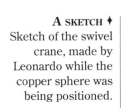

A SKETCH ♦
Sketch of the swivel crane, made by Leonardo while the copper sphere was being positioned.

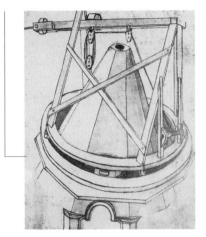

BUONACCORSO ♦ GHIBERTI
Another drawing of the swivel crane, by Buonaccorso Ghiberti, an engineer and contemporary of Leonardo.

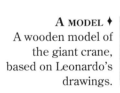

♦ INSIDE THE DOME
A drawing of the crane as it would have stood inside the dome.

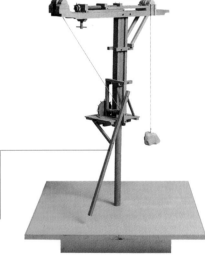

A MODEL ♦
A wooden model of the giant crane, based on Leonardo's drawings.

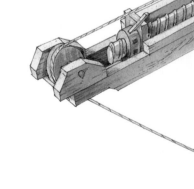

THE BIG CRANE ♦
For raising loads from the base of the dome to the platform, Filippo Brunelleschi had designed a huge jib crane, similar to those used on modern building sites. Below right is a wooden model of the crane.

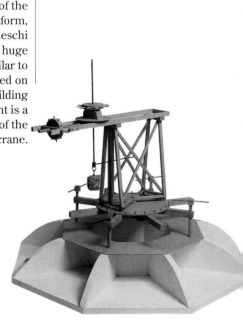

☞ *As a child, Leonardo had learned to observe the natural world. Verrocchio introduced him to the world of machines and technology. In his workshop Leonardo watched the building of the great copper sphere that was to crown the dome of the cathedral, but what particularly fascinated him were the enormous engines designed to lift and manoeuvre this heavy object safely. On May 27, 1471, when the sphere was eventually fixed in place, Leonardo was there taking notes. Throughout his life, in his search to understand how things worked, Leonardo made notes and drawings on subjects from anatomy and botany to astronomy and mechanics. Over three thousand pages of his notebooks have been preserved. Leonardo was left-handed and wrote in an unusual way: from right to left, with the letters the wrong way round. This is known as mirror writing. The way to decipher it is to hold his pages of notes in front of a mirror.* ☞

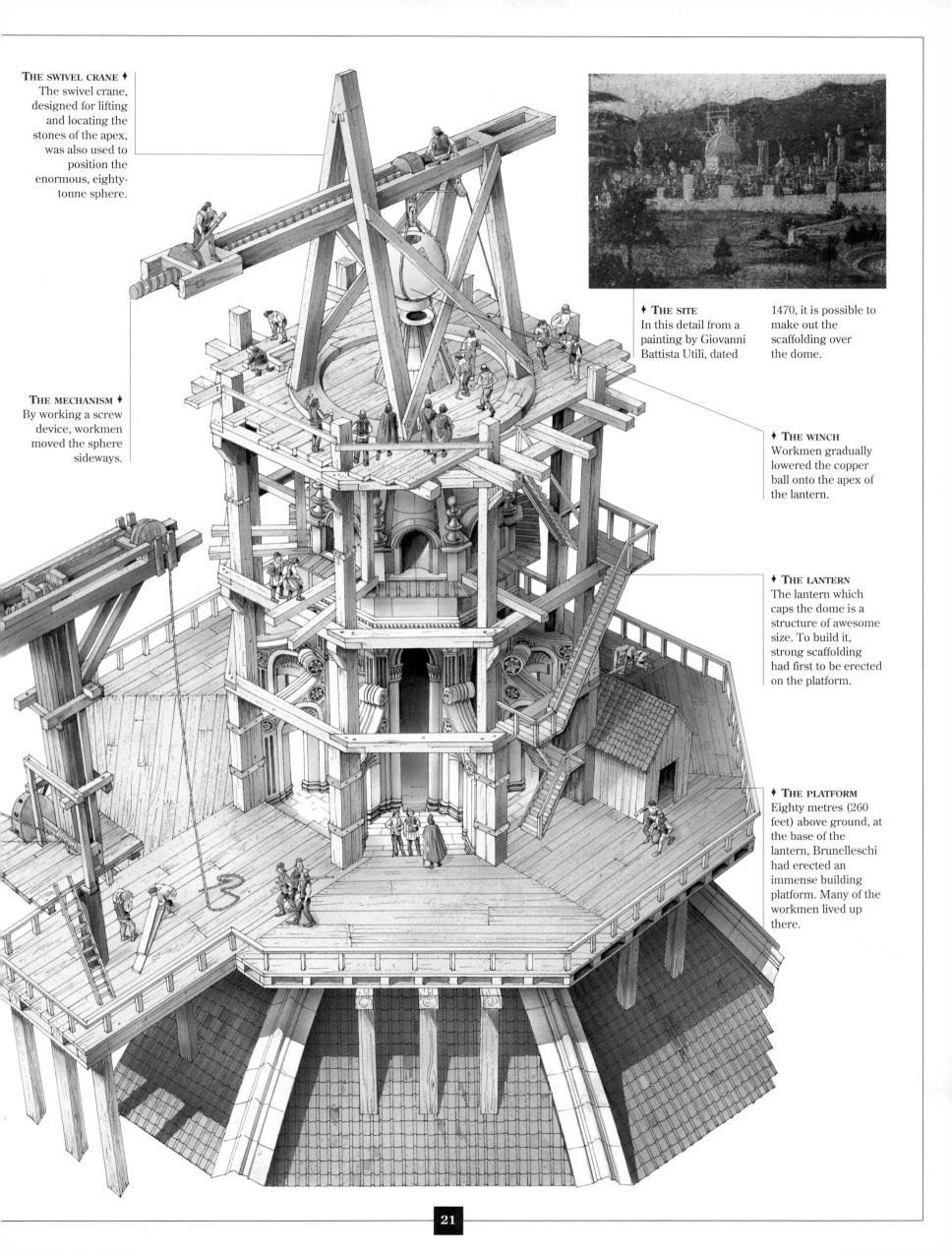

THE SWIVEL CRANE ✦
The swivel crane, designed for lifting and locating the stones of the apex, was also used to position the enormous, eighty-tonne sphere.

THE MECHANISM ✦
By working a screw device, workmen moved the sphere sideways.

✦ THE SITE
In this detail from a painting by Giovanni Battista Utili, dated 1470, it is possible to make out the scaffolding over the dome.

✦ THE WINCH
Workmen gradually lowered the copper ball onto the apex of the lantern.

✦ THE LANTERN
The lantern which caps the dome is a structure of awesome size. To build it, strong scaffolding had first to be erected on the platform.

✦ THE PLATFORM
Eighty metres (260 feet) above ground, at the base of the lantern, Brunelleschi had erected an immense building platform. Many of the workmen lived up there.

Bronze Casting

In the Middle Ages there was no attempt to cast large bronze statues of the kind made by the Greeks and Romans. However, the technique of bronze casting was still used in the making of bells. Master bell-founders had kept the tradition alive, and in the fourteenth century their knowledge was put to use in the casting of cannon. When Florentine sculptors such as Ghiberti and Donatello turned their hand to large bronze statues, the experience of the bell-founders was invaluable. Verrocchio, too, drew on their skills, and eventually became famous throughout Italy for his ability in casting bronze. In his workshop he set up a full-scale foundry, and there Leonardo learned the rudiments of the technique.

♦ David
A bronze statue cast by Verrocchio around 1465.

♦ 1. The model
The first stage in the "lost wax" process of bronze casting: the sculptor makes a clay model.

♦ 2. The copy
The sculptor then makes a copy of the model, building up a shell of wax over a metal framework. The thickness of the wax determines the final thickness of the bronze.

☞ *In 1472 Leonardo was enrolled in the Corporation of St Luke - the painters' guild - but continued his training with Verrocchio. His master was best known as a sculptor, accomplished in all techniques. From him Leonardo learned that art is first and foremost an intellectual activity. He was encouraged to make a careful and systematic study of a subject he intended to reproduce in painting or sculpture. He learned that to sculpt a convincing figure, it was first necessary to make models. Following Verrocchio's instructions, he spent a lot of time modelling the faces of children. The complicated procedures of bronze casting fascinated him. He began to acquire the technical concepts that awakened his interest in science. In 1476, at the age of twenty-four, Leonardo left Verrocchio's workshop. But when his former master received a commission to make a great equestrian monument, Leonardo was quick to offer his assistance.* ☞

♦ Doubting Thomas
A bronze group from the artist's later years, completed by Verrocchio in 1483.

3. Ducts ♦
When the figure is completed, the sculptor fits wax tubes to the wax outer shell. When he comes to cast the statue, these serve as ducts for pouring the bronze and venting air.

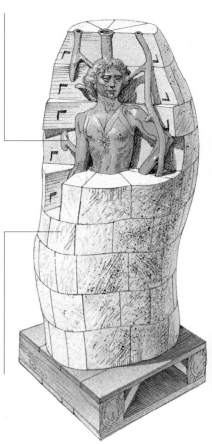

4. The mould ♦
The sculptor then makes a heat-resistant plaster mould - a sort of "negative" of the statue. This outer casing is tightly held together with strong iron bands.

♦ Winged "putto"
This bronze sculpture, by Verrocchio, can be seen in the courtyard of the Palazzo Vecchio, Florence.

8. Removing the ♦ plaster
When the bronze has cooled, workmen break off the plaster mould with hammer and chisel. The unfinished statue emerges, the ducts now consisting of solid bronze.

9. Finishing ♦
The ducts are now sawn off and the sculptor can put the finishing touches to his work: trimming off excess metal, correcting any mistakes, engraving decorative features, and finally polishing the statue.

♦ 5. MELTING THE WAX
The mould is heated in a special oven, until all the wax melts and runs out. This creates the empty space that will be filled by the molten bronze.

♦ THE RISKS
Casting was a difficult and dangerous operation: difficult, because any change in the temperature or weather might make the process go wrong; dangerous, because any humidity in the mould could cause an explosion.

6. CASTING ♦
From the furnace, molten bronze is poured into the mould through a funnel-shaped opening.

7. BURYING THE ♦ MOULD
The mould is buried, to prevent the heat of the molten bronze causing it to explode.

♦ LIFTING
The mould is lifted and manoeuvred using a winch and strong tackle.

♦ THE ANVIL
The metal bands used for holding the mould together are forged on the anvil.

THE EQUESTRIAN MONUMENT

Renowned for his skills as a sculptor and caster of bronze, in 1476 Verrocchio received a most desirable commission from the republic of Venice: to fashion an equestrian monument to the soldier of fortune Bartolomeo Colleoni. It was to be a statue of exceptional size, no less than four metres (13 feet) high. Since Roman times, only Donatello had dared undertake so difficult a task. The project galvanized the whole workshop. Verrocchio's team had to make dozens of preliminary drawings, prepare models of various sizes on which to study the problems they would encounter in the actual casting, and show the client what the monument would eventually look like. From the small-scale models, they would progress to a full-sized one, make from it a gigantic mould, and finally cast the statue. Leonardo's involvement in the project led him to want to produce an equestrian monument of his own. And many years later the ruler of Milan asked him to cast a horse seven metres (23 feet) high.

STUDY ✦
Leonardo made this sketch sometime between 1508 and 1511.

THE CAGE FOR ✦ THE MODEL
The model was installed in a cage. Thin rods were inserted through holes in the woodwork, as a way of measuring the distance between the cage and the various parts of the model.

THE CAGE FOR ✦ THE STATUE
A second cage was built, double the size of the original. Inside this cage the full-sized statue was modelled. To achieve the correct dimensions, rods were again used to measure the distances between statue and cage.

✦WORKING OUTSIDE
The statue was to be installed in an open square. To gauge the effect of natural light, it had to be worked on out of doors.

👉 *Leonardo's first major paintings - the* Annunciation *or his panel painting of the* Adoration of the Magi *- took up only part of his time. When he was not busy, he would visit the fascinating laboratory of Tommaso Masini, nicknamed Zoroastro, a craftsman skilled in foundry work and mechanical and hydraulic engineering. Leonardo designed bridges, hydraulic devices and military machines; Zoroastro would faithfully reproduce them as scale models. Concerns on the part of Leonardo's father that his son lacked application were soon laid to rest by Leonardo's diligence and enthusiasm in studying the anatomy of the horse. At this time, Leonardo produced a host of drawings of horses' heads, hocks and manes. His immediate intention was to help Verrocchio with his monument, but gradually he began to nurture an ambition that stayed with him for the rest of his life: to design and cast a huge equestrian monument of his own.* 👉

♦ WORK IN PROGRESS
The monument was modelled some distance off the ground, bearing in mind the position it would eventually occupy.

♦ SCAFFOLDING
The monument was designed to stand well off the ground. So that the sculptor could assess its impact when seen from below, it was mounted on tall scaffolding.

♦ PROTECTION
At night and on rainy days, the monument was covered with canvas sheets.

ADORATION OF THE MAGI

According to the gospels, shepherds were sent by a heavenly host of angels to worship the infant Jesus; they were followed by astrologers from the East, who had been guided by a star. Departing from tradition, Leonardo depicted the scene in quite a different way. His composition shows a great crowd arranged in a semi-circle around the Virgin and Child, while horsemen fight among the ruins in the background.

◆ MASACCIO
In this painting from 1426 - Staatliche Museen, Berlin - Masaccio followed a traditional pattern: the procession of worshippers is arranged parallel to the picture plane.

THE WORK
Antimony yellow with green earth, bistre and white lead, 246 x 243 cm (8 x 8 feet). Uffizi Gallery, Florence. In 1481 the monks of San Donato a Scopeto commissioned Leonardo to paint an altar-piece of the *Adoration of the Magi*. The work was to be completed in two and a half years, but Leonardo did not meet the deadline and, on his departure for Milan, the painting remained unfinished. Fifteen years later, the monks gave up and commissioned another version of the scene by Filippino Lippi. Above and below are three

preparatory drawings for Leonardo's painting. Executed towards the end of his first stay in Florence, the work was experimental in composition and technique. It belonged to the Medici collections in the early seventeenth century, but was already at the Uffizi in 1670, though not exhibited until 1794.

Leonardo's technique is easy to analyze in this picture, because he left it unfinished. We can make out the stages of his work, from the bare outlines of the Virgin to the more or less completed figure on the right. Leonardo drew the scene with a brush and *green earth. In modelling the figures, he used bistre for the darker areas and let the underpainting show through for the lighter tones. After painting the foreground in brown, he returned to the figures, using blacks and touches of white.*

◆ IMPROVISATION
Leonardo did not follow a set pattern but allowed his creative genius free rein. It is unusual to find in a painting the immediacy of expression characteristic of drawing.

♦ **ALMOST FINISHED**
These figures, first modelled in chiaroscuro (light and shade), then given added contrast with black and highlights of white, lack only the final touches of colour.

BOTTICELLI ♦
In his *Adoration of the Magi* of 1480 - Uffizi Gallery, Florence - Botticelli arranged his subjects on either side of the picture so that the eye is drawn in to the centre.

♦ **A PREPARATORY DRAWING**
In a grandiose setting of classical ruins, horsemen and warriors engage in battle. They symbolize human conflict, in opposition to the reign of peace brought by the infant Christ. The roof supported by the ruins probably symbolizes the Church arising out of the chaos of the pagan world. This feature was not carried over into the final painting.

♦ **CONTRAST**
The emphasis on dark colours makes the lighter tones stand out all the more clearly, and this produces a three-dimensional quality. Here, Leonardo comes close to the light-and-shade effects of sculpture.

FILIPPINO LIPPI ♦
Completed in 1496 in place of Leonardo's painting, Filippino Lippi's *Adoration* - Uffizi Gallery, Florence - is composed on similar lines, but lacks the complexity of Leonardo's work.

THE MEDICIS

Fifteenth-century Italy was a mosaic of petty kingdoms, principalities, dominions and city-states, often in conflict with one another. Some, like Naples and Milan, were ruled by kings or dukes. Others had a republican form of government, for instance Venice, Siena and Genoa. Florence was also nominally a republic, but in fact the city was dominated by a rich and powerful family of bankers: the Medicis. They rarely held public office, but from their palace pulled strings to direct the affairs of the state. When they gave advice, it was treated as an order, and they ensured that the levers of power were controlled by people they could trust. In 1469 Lorenzo de' Medici became head of the family. His abilities as a statesman and his love of the arts earned him the nickname of "the Magnificent". In politics he displayed intelligence and caution. Knowing that Florence could not compete with stronger states on the battlefield, he sought to maintain peace: forming alliances, lending money and making gifts. He cultivated close relations with artists. As well as sponsoring works of art to beautify the city, Lorenzo used artists as instruments of diplomacy, effectively lending them to the rulers of other cities in exchange for political favours.

♦ THE MEDICIS

The Medicis were a family of rich country landowners, who subsequently moved to Florence. They engaged in trade and soon became involved in banking. Having acquired great wealth, they began to be influential in the political life of the city. They became dominant in the time of Cosimo il Vecchio, Lorenzo's grandfather. It was Cosimo, rather than Lorenzo, who commissioned many of Florence's magnificent new buildings: the church of San Lorenzo, the convent of San Marco, and the Palazzo Medici-Riccardi itself. The Medicis were to dominate the city for centuries. The last member of the dynasty, Gian Gastone, died without heir in the eighteenth century.

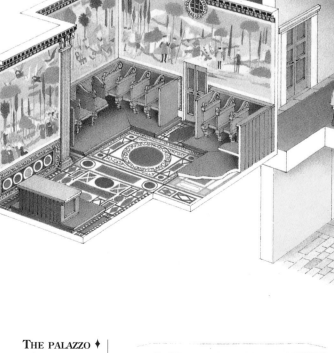

THE ITALIAN STATES ♦
In the second half of the fifteenth century, Italy was divided into many petty states.

1 PIEDMONT
2 MONTFERRAT
3 SALUZZO
4 GENOA
5 MILAN
6 VENETIAN REPUBLIC
7 MANTUA
8 FERRARA
9 MODENA
10 PAPAL STATES
11 LUCCA
12 FLORENCE
13 SIENA
14 KINGDOM OF NAPLES

FRESCOES ♦
At the heart of the Medici residence, the chapel was richly decorated by Benozzo Gozzoli in 1459. His frescoes glorified the Medicis, including portraits of the founder and other members of the dynasty.

THE PALAZZO ♦
The Medici residence in via Larga was designed and built in the years 1444 to 1459 by the architect Michelozzo.

THE COURTYARD ♦
The palace was built around an open courtyard, its elegant loggia supported on classical columns.

♦ A MEDICI PARTY
This miniature by Apollonio di Giovanni, painted in 1460, shows a party in the garden of the Palazzo Medici-Riccardi.

☞ As one of Verrocchio's brightest pupils, and the son of an influential supporter of the Medici family, Leonardo did not long escape the attention of Lorenzo the Magnificent. He was a frequent visitor at the Medici residence in via Larga, where he met artists, poets and scholars, and he carried out restoration work on sculptures in the Medici gardens near the piazza San Marco. At the same time he continued to paint. Then an unexpected turn of events gave him the opportunity to leave Florence and move to the rich and powerful city of Milan. Lorenzo had been promising the lords of Milan - the Sforza family - that he would send a Florentine artist to cast an impressive equestrian monument to the memory of Francesco Sforza, soldier of fortune and founder of the dynasty. The choice fell on Leonardo. Leaving the Adoration of the Magi *unfinished*, Leonardo set out for Milan. ☞

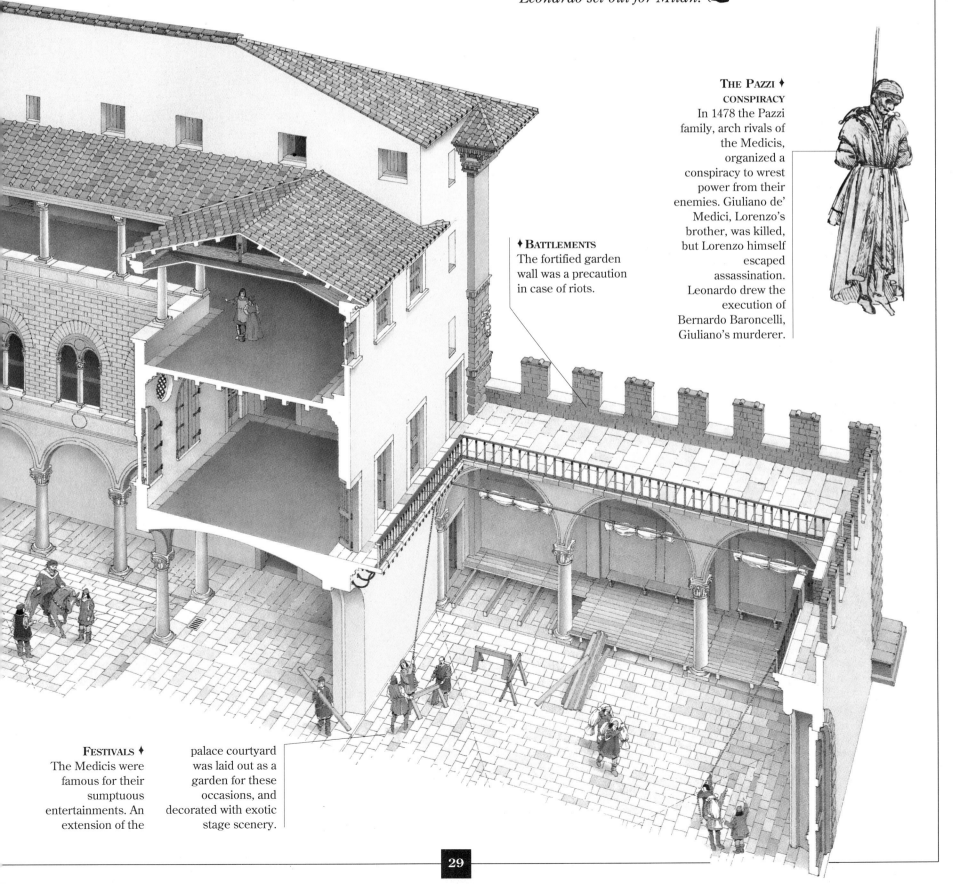

THE PAZZI ♦
CONSPIRACY
In 1478 the Pazzi family, arch rivals of the Medicis, organized a conspiracy to wrest power from their enemies. Giuliano de' Medici, Lorenzo's brother, was killed, but Lorenzo himself escaped assassination. Leonardo drew the execution of Bernardo Baroncelli, Giuliano's murderer.

♦ BATTLEMENTS
The fortified garden wall was a precaution in case of riots.

FESTIVALS ♦
The Medicis were famous for their sumptuous entertainments. An extension of the palace courtyard was laid out as a garden for these occasions, and decorated with exotic stage scenery.

MILAN

When Leonardo entered the service of Ludovico Sforza, he was thirty years old. Milan was a very different place from Florence. Ludovico, known as "Il Moro" (the Moor), was an absolute ruler and lived in an immense fortress, a city within the city. His power rested on a large army, equipped with the most modern weapons available. Milan was famous throughout Europe for the production of armaments, and there were foundries and metal-working shops in every street. The Milanese were open to new ideas: silk-worm culture had recently been established, and textile businesses were prospering thanks to the invention of advanced new weaving looms. Farmers were just beginning to experiment with growing rice, and irrigation canals were being dug in the surrounding countryside. Because of Ludovico's insatiable thirst for prestige, Milan offered great opportunities to artists and men of science. The seventeen years Leonardo spent there were a time of growth, during which he was fully engaged on many works and projects.

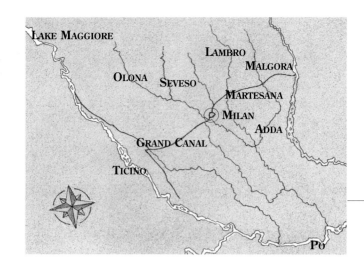

LAKE MAGGIORE — OLONA — SEVESO — LAMBRO — MALGORA — MARTESANA — MILAN — ADDA — GRAND CANAL — TICINO — Po

♦ **CANALS**
The dense network of canals around Milan was used for transporting goods and raw materials from the region of the Italian lakes and the River Po. For the construction of the castle, timber was brought from the Alps, bricks from the surrounding countryside, and cement from Lake Maggiore.

♦ **CECILIA GALLERANI**
The mistress of Ludovico il Moro. She took a special interest in Leonardo.

♦ **FRANCESCO DI GIORGIO MARTINI**
A great architect and engineer, with whom Leonardo became friends. He gave Leonardo a precious manuscript containing drawings of machines and architectural projects.

♦ **LA ROCCHETTA**
The Rocchetta courtyard, like the Duke's courtyard, was built to the orders of Galeazzo Maria Visconti.

♦ **BLANCHE OF SAVOY TOWER**
The stronghold in which Ludovico il Moro imprisoned his sister-in-law.

♦ **THE CASTLE**
The first part of the castle was built in 1368 under Duke Galeazzo Visconti. It incorporated part of the city wall.

♦ **THE SFORZAS**
On the death of Filippo Maria Visconti in 1447, the people of Milan rose up and proclaimed a republic. The castle was partially destroyed. In 1450 Francesco Sforza seized the dukedom of Milan and began an ambitious programme of rebuilding and extending the fortress. This work was continued by his successors: Galeazzo Maria Sforza and Ludovico il Moro. They engaged some of the greatest contemporary architects: Filarete, Bramante, and Leonardo.

THE MODEL ♦
In 1493, to mark the marriage of Maria Sforza, the clay model of Leonardo's horse was exhibited in the centre of the "great court".

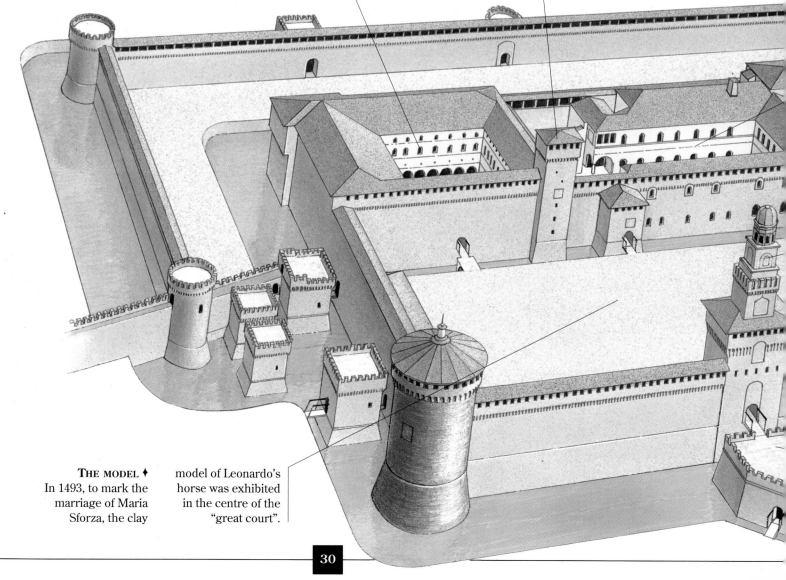

♦ A COMPARISON

Leonardo's horse (4) would have towered over: 1) the Roman statue of *Marcus Aurelius*, 4.30 metres (14 feet) high; 2) Donatello's *Gattamelata* in Padua, 3.20 metres (10.5 feet); 3) Verrocchio's *Colleoni* in Venice, 4 metres (13 feet); 5) Girardon's *Louis XIV* in Paris, 6.82 metres (22 feet).

♦ THE MONUMENT

Leonardo had come to Milan to create an equestrian monument in memory of Duke Francesco, founder of the Sforza dynasty. He worked on the project for some ten years. His plans were daring: the monument would be larger than any existing work of its kind. The horse alone would stand six

metres (19 feet 8 inches) high. Having made preliminary drawings and produced a number of proposals, he got as far as building a life-sized model of the horse, which was displayed in the great court of the castle. He studied possible methods of casting the statue, and designed colossal engines for moving

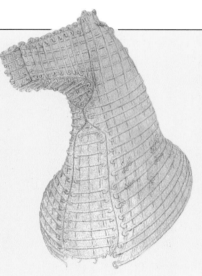

the model and the planned bronze horse. He devised a system for boxing the mould and, helped by his mathematician friend Luca Pacioli, calculated how much bronze would be required. However, when French troops captured Milan in 1499, they destroyed the model, viewing it as a symbol of Sforza ambition.

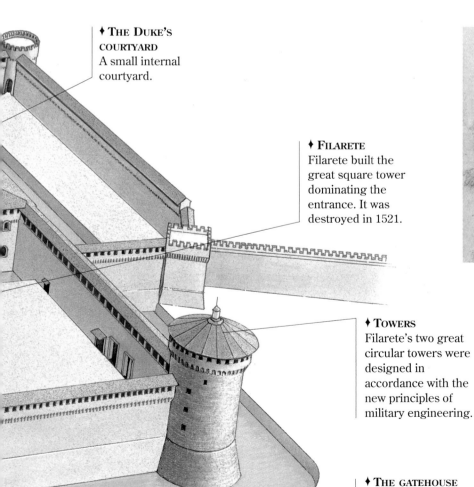

♦ THE DUKE'S COURTYARD
A small internal courtyard.

♦ FILARETE
Filarete built the great square tower dominating the entrance. It was destroyed in 1521.

♦ TOWERS
Filarete's two great circular towers were designed in accordance with the new principles of military engineering.

♦ THE GATEHOUSE
The gatehouse protects the entrance to the castle. This is where the equestrian monument was intended to stand.

♦ CELEBRATIONS
Leonardo played many roles at the Milanese court: painter, sculptor, military and hydraulic engineer, architect, and even master of ceremonies. Contemporaries praised his organization of festivities, and some of his drawings for the costumes have survived.

☞ *Having studied the anatomy of the horse so thoroughly under Verrocchio, Leonardo was impatient to create an equestrian monument of his own. But the first call on his services was as a musician. Lorenzo had asked for Leonardo's beautiful silver lyre, and sent it to Ludovico together with its maker and player. In the spring of 1482 Leonardo addressed a letter of introduction to his new patron, listing his skills in mechanics, hydraulics and military engineering, as well as painting and sculpture, in which he claimed to be second to none. Ludovico's curiosity was aroused by an artist who dared deal on equal terms with the lord of Milan. He therefore sent for him, to see if he was really a madman with an inflated idea of himself, or a true creative genius.* ☞

THE VIRGIN OF THE ROCKS

The story goes that, while Mary and Joseph were fleeing to Egypt with Jesus to save him from the anger of king Herod, they found refuge in a cave in the Sinai desert. There occurred a miraculous first meeting between Jesus and John the Baptist, whom Leonardo depicts as little more than babies. St John is portrayed as kneeling to receive the blessing of his cousin. This little-known episode from the life of Christ is not related in the gospels, but in later - apocryphal - books, to which the Church ascribed a lesser status.

♦ THE SECOND VERSION ♦
Completed ten years after the first *Virgin of the Rocks*, the London painting shows the same scene, although the figures are proportionally larger. The only difference is that the angel in this version is not shown as pointing to St John.

♦ THE PAINTING
Oil on wooden panel, 199 x 122 cm (6.5 x 4 feet). Louvre, Paris. In 1483 the Brotherhood of the Immaculate Conception commissioned Leonardo to paint an altar-piece for their chapel in the church of San Francesco Grande in Milan. The work was to be flanked by two other panels and a number of painted bas-reliefs by Ambrogio and

Evangelista De Predis. Above and below are preparatory drawings for the work which was painted between 1483 and 1486. It seems never to have occupied its intended position, but found its way eventually to the Louvre. Instead, the altar was graced with a second version of the subject, which Leonardo finished around 1507. This is now in the National Gallery, London.

As the diagram above illustrates, there are two different light sources in this picture. Leonardo observed that light is present, in different degrees, in all parts of the atmosphere. Because a single light source creates over-sharp contrasts, and Leonardo wished to achieve a softer "sfumato" *effect, he imagined the main source of light as being in front of his subjects, with a second, weaker source in the background. "Sfumato" means blending one colour area subtly into the next.*

AN EXPERT IN ♦ BOTANY
Fascinated since childhood by the wonders of the natural world, Leonardo studied plant species with the enthusiasm of a botanist.

♦ **TRANSPARENT EFFECTS**
Leonardo achieved transparent effects of great delicacy by applying thin coats of boiled walnut oil. The light appears to penetrate gradually into the depths of the painting.

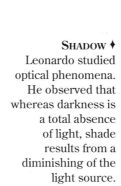

SHADOW ♦
Leonardo studied optical phenomena. He observed that whereas darkness is a total absence of light, shade results from a diminishing of the light source.

♦ **HANDS**
Gestures are vital in conveying the meaning of this silent scene. The angel is pointing to St John, whose hands are joined in prayer in recognition of Jesus, the appointed Redeemer. The Christchild in turn blesses the prophet who is to herald his coming. The Virgin extends her hand in a gesture of protection.

♦ **THE ROCKS**
In his *Treatise on Painting*, Leonardo stated that the arid, rugged summits of mountains should be represented with "small, stunted vegetation" and roots emerging from the dry earth. Towards the valley, the plant life should gradually become more luxuriant.

PLANT LIFE ♦
The iris in the left foreground, and all the other flowers and plants represented in the painting, are drawn from nature.

ARCHITECTURE

The principles of the new building style that Brunelleschi and Alberti had pioneered in Florence were spreading to other Italian cities. In Milan, Ludovico invited forward-looking architects to undertake the major task of transforming an old medieval city into an ideal modern metropolis. Between 1460 and 1465 Antonio Averulino, nicknamed Filarete, built the Ospedale Maggiore, a prototype of later European hospitals. In 1473 Lazzaro Palazzi built the first isolation hospital. Donato Bramante, Francesco di Giorgio and Antonio Amadeo designed churches, convents, town houses, and chapels. The fashion for symmetrical buildings with a central plan - a classical idea taken up by Brunelleschi - also caught on in Milan. Meanwhile, engineers were engaged to construct a dense network of inland waterways. This was the climate in which Leonardo embarked on a series of architectural studies, none of which was ever realized. His most ambitious project anticipates many of the principles of modern town planning.

♦ SANTA MARIA PRESSO SANTO SATIRO
This church was one of Bramante's first achievements in Milan (1483).

BRAMANTE ♦
Bramante already enjoyed great prestige when he arrived in Milan in 1480. He dedicated a poem on Roman architecture to Leonardo.

L'OSPEDALE ♦ MAGGIORE
Milan's new hospital was designed by the architect Antonio Averulino, nicknamed Filarete (1400-1469). The grandiose and orderly lay-out of the building was much admired by Leonardo.

♦ A NEW RESIDENTIAL AREA
Leonardo drew plans for rebuilding the old heart of Milan. A severe outbreak of plague had revealed the terrible lack of hygiene in the area. Leonardo was the first to insist on proper sanitation.

♦ ARCADES
Pedestrian streets were protected from the rain by arcades.

♦ A RATIONAL VIEW
In Leonardo's day many of the cities of northern Italy were served by a network of canals, most of which have now disappeared. Milan had much in common with Venice, Amsterdam or Bruges. Leonardo came from Tuscany, a region poor in water resources, and he was fascinated by the busy canals, the boats laden with merchandise, and the way the buildings were mirrored in the water. He realized that water could be utilized in a more rational way: for transport, hygiene, and to enhance the urban environment.

RAISED ROADWAYS ♦
Leonardo made a separation between pedestrian areas and roads intended to carry traffic.

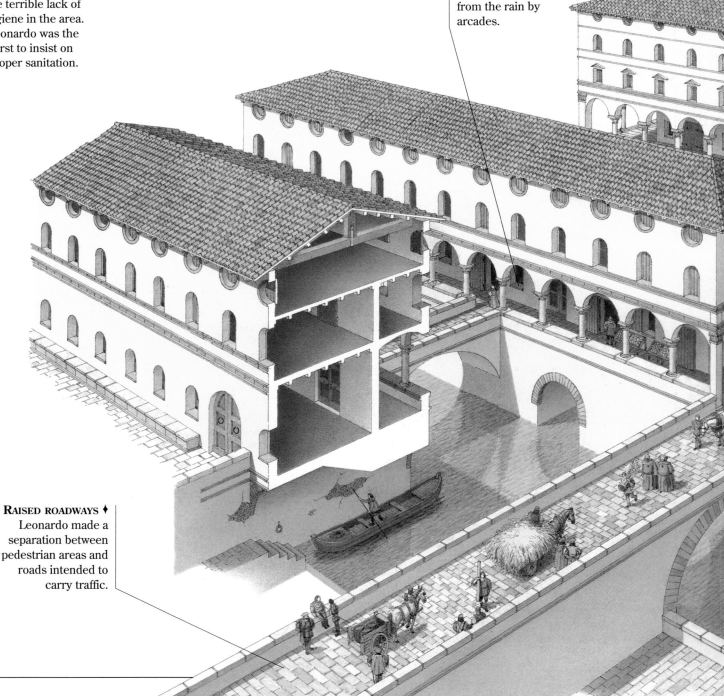

♦ BUILDING TO A CENTRAL PLAN
Renaissance architects were fascinated by geometry, and saw buildings as skilful combinations of geometrical shapes. The most perfect were the square and the circle, the cube and the sphere. They therefore devoted special attention to centrally-planned buildings which would fit into a circle or a square. Leonardo showed a great deal of interest in the new developments. He drew up plans for a number of symmetrical churches, but unfortunately they were never built.

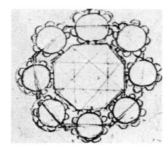

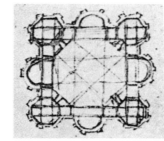

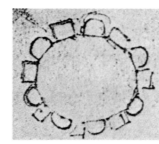

☞ *Ludovico granted Leonardo an annual allowance of five hundred ducats. Whilst waiting to build the promised war machines and the gigantic equestrian monument, the artist painted such major works as the* Virgin of the Rocks *and a portrait of Cecilia Gallerani, entitled* Lady with an Ermine. *But Leonardo's mind was particularly stimulated by the enthusiasm for architecture that had taken hold of the city. He knew and worked with such great architects as Bramante and Francesco di Giorgio. There had been much discussion of what would constitute a suitable dome for Milan's cathedral, and Leonardo, too, submitted a project. With scientific rigour he elaborated plans for enlarging Milan, and designed a canal network linking two rivers. Even an outbreak of the plague did not distract him from his many research projects. On the contrary, it gave him the opportunity to work undisturbed.* ☜

♦ BUILDINGS
The buildings were designed on several levels, with access to waterways, roads and pedestrian walkways.

♦ THE CATHEDRAL
Leonardo produced some brilliant studies of how a dome might be added to Milan cathedral.

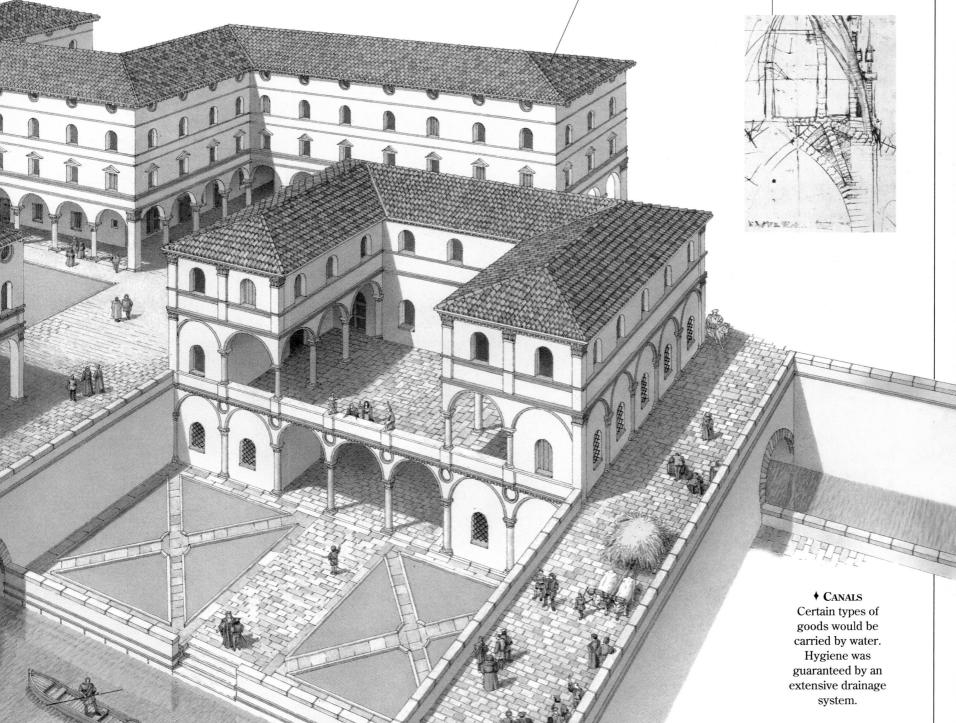

♦ CANALS
Certain types of goods would be carried by water. Hygiene was guaranteed by an extensive drainage system.

ANATOMY

Even before 1400 Italian painters and sculptors had made careful studies of the human body so as to reproduce it faithfully in their art. During the Renaissance a growing concern for realism involved artists in more detailed and painstaking anatomical research. They wanted to understand and represent the movement of the limbs, muscles under stress, and facial expressions. To further their understanding, many dissected dead bodies, first in secret, then more openly. Leonardo was no exception. However, his drawings reveal that he took a scientific, as well as a purely artistic, interest in the subject. His studies of the muscles, nervous and vascular systems, and of the skeleton are fine examples of what we would call scientific drawing. Thirty or forty years later, Andreas Vesalius (1514-1564), a Flemish anatomist and surgeon, published magnificent illustrations of the human skeleton, which mark the real beginning of modern anatomy.

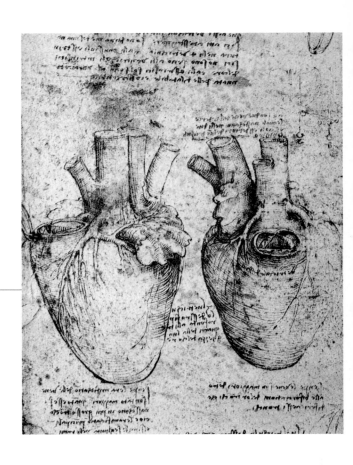

THE HEART ✦
Leonardo's annotated diagrams of the cardiac muscle (right). The anatomical characteristics are well defined, though Leonardo had not fully understood how the heart works. At the top left of this page is the famous diagram showing the proportions of the human body, which Leonardo took from the Roman architect Vitruvius.

✦ DISSECTION
To gain the precise understanding of the human body which his drawings show, Leonardo carried out as many as thirty dissections.

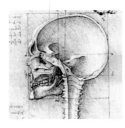

✦ THE HEAD
These three drawings by Leonardo show the skull,

a cross-section of the head, and the structure of the neck.

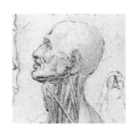

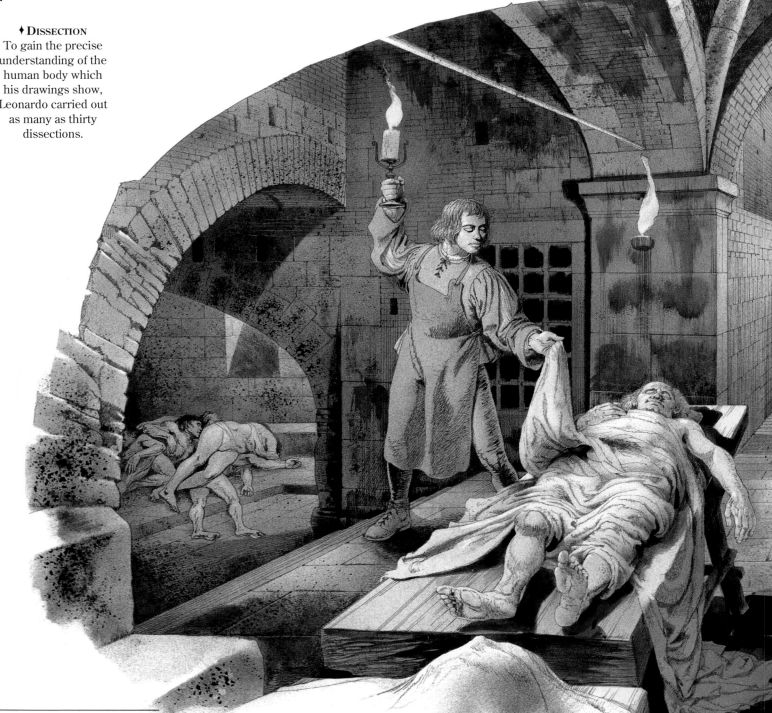

THE THORAX ♦
This drawing of the thoracic and abdominal organs was made around 1512, when Leonardo was studying with the Paduan scientist Della Torre. The kidneys and urinary system are accurately reproduced, the result of direct observation of dissected bodies.

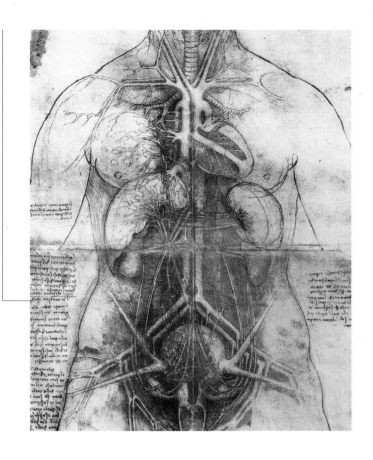

The years went by, but still Leonardo had not begun casting the horse, for which Lorenzo the Magnificent had first sent him to Milan. Ludovico occasionally reproved him, and complained of the delay to the Florentine ambassador. Leonardo's response was to re-immerse himself in his studies but, being a perfectionist, he often changed his mind and began all over again. In 1489 Ludovico asked Lorenzo to send two master foundrymen to begin work on the monument. Meanwhile Leonardo continued to create the scenery for court entertainments. In 1490 he built elaborate stage sets for the marriage of Gian Galeazzo Sforza to Isabella of Aragon, representing paradise and seven orbiting planets. Another distraction was Leonardo's growing interest in the study of anatomy. Originally motivated by an artistic impulse, he soon became involved in scientific classification, driven by his insatiable curiosity. His drawings are natural and realistic, even when he depicts anatomical features of his own invention.

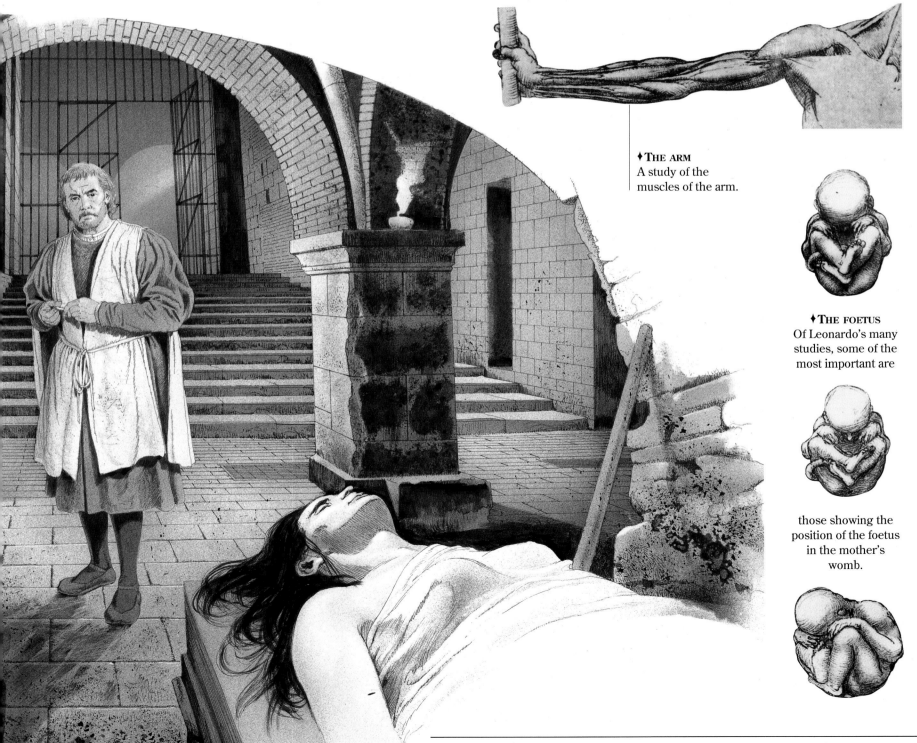

♦ THE ARM
A study of the muscles of the arm.

♦ THE FOETUS
Of Leonardo's many studies, some of the most important are

those showing the position of the foetus in the mother's womb.

PORTRAITS

♦ PORTRAITS
The portrait of *Ginevra de' Benci* (National Gallery of Art, Washington), oil on wooden panel, 42 x 37 cm (16.5 x 14.5 inches), has affinities with Flemish portraits, which Leonardo would have seen in Florentine collections. Similar in composition and lighting are three portraits painted by Leonardo at the court of Ludovico il Moro in 1485-1490: *Portrait of a Musician* (Pinacoteca Ambrosiana, Milan),

oil on wooden panel, 44 x 42 cm (17 x 16.5 inches); *Cecilia Gallerani* (Czartoryski Museum, Cracow), oil on wooden panel, 55 x 40 cm (21.5 x 15.5 inches); and the so-called *Belle Ferronnière* (Louvre, Paris), oil on wooden panel, 63 x 45 cm (25 x 18 inches). In 1490 Leonardo sketched *La Scapigliata* (Pinacoteca Nazionale, Parma), 25 x 21 cm (10 x 8 inches), a girl with undressed hair, bowed head and gaze directed down. In 1500 he drew a fine profile of *Isabella d'Este* (Louvre, Paris), charcoal and pastel on paper, 63 x 46 cm (25 x 18 inches). A preparatory drawing is shown above.

Leonardo painted many portraits of women, including the best-known *Mona Lisa* (left); but only one of a man. Whereas artists before him had portrayed women in the abstract, representing an ideal of beauty, Leonardo endowed them with personality, force of character, and social status. He managed to combine a spirited physical description with considerable psychological insight. As in a modern puzzle, he sometimes included symbols - objects, plants or animals - suggesting the name of his subject and alluding to her moral qualities.

♦ THE EMBLEM
A branch of juniper flanked by laurel and palm are bound by a scroll with a Latin motto: "Beauty is the ornament of Virtue".

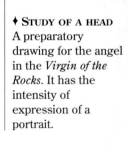

♦ STUDY OF A HEAD
A preparatory drawing for the angel in the *Virgin of the Rocks*. It has the intensity of expression of a portrait.

Ginevra de' Benci, sister of an astronomer friend of Leonardo's, was married at the age of seventeen. Her portrait (above), painted in 1474 for the occasion, reveals a pale young woman with adolescent features, gazing sadly into *the distance. The juniper bush in the background symbolizes the chastity of a young bride. The Italian word for juniper, "ginepro", also suggests her name. On the reverse of the portrait is an emblem, as shown top right.*

THE BENOIS ♦ MADONNA
Painted during Leonardo's first stay in Florence, this Madonna, spontaneously playing with her baby, has the lively, light-hearted quality of an adolescent.

The subject's gaze is
directed slightly
above and to the right
of the observer,
creating the
impression of an
ambiguous, evasive
personality.

✦ CECILIA GALLERANI
Ludovico's mistress,
a woman of wit and
beauty, who for many
years shone at the
Milanese court. The
severe hair-style
emphasizes the
perfection of her face
and striking eyes.
The white ermine she
holds is a symbol of
purity; its name in
Greek suggests her
name.

**PORTRAIT OF A
MUSICIAN ✦**
Leonardo's only male
portrait. Although the
clothing and hand
holding the musical
score (not shown
here) were left
unfinished, the face is
highly expressive.

✦ LADY WITH PEARLS
The rigid profile and
rather fixed
expression are quite
unlike the other
portraits. Though
long thought to be by
Leonardo, this is now
recognized as a
painting of the
Bolognese school.

ISABELLA D'ESTE ✦
The head of the
Marchioness of
Mantua is seen in
profile, while the bust
remains rigidly
turned towards the
viewer, suggesting an
important person
with a strong
personality. Although
she insisted for years,
Leonardo never
fulfilled her request
for a portrait of
herself to hang in her
study. The bust and
hands of this portrait
are reminiscent of the
Mona Lisa.

✦ LA SCAPIGLIATA
(Lady with Hair
Undone). This
splendid face, a study
for the angel in the
Virgin of the Rocks, or
possibly a sketch for
the long-awaited
portrait of Isabella
d'Este, expresses
youthful melancholy
and reflection.

Mathematics

In 1453, when the Ottoman Turks conquered Constantinople, many Byzantine scholars sought refuge in Italy, taking with them precious Greek manuscripts. These included treatises on geometry. At the same time the German Johannes Gutenberg was perfecting the technique of printing with moveable type (originally a Chinese invention), so making books more widely available. These two developments are closely related to the spread of mathematical knowledge. Another factor was the great voyages of discovery. Sailors needed accurate nautical charts, precise tables for predicting their position, and better ways of making astronomical calculations. Sophisticated accounting systems were developed as trade flourished. Artists also made a contribution to science, with the invention of perspective. At this time mathematicians played an important role in the spread of algebra and geometry. An influential figure was Luca Pacioli. Leonardo is said to have drawn the polygons for Pacioli's *De divina proportione*, a treatise on geometry.

♦ REGIOMONTANUS
Johann Müller of Königsberg, known as Regiomontanus (1436-1476), was the most accomplished mathematician of his time. He studied in Leipzig and Vienna, and in Rome learned Greek, in order to read the classical texts on mathematics.

♦ NEW UNDERSTANDING
The spread of scientific knowledge continued throughout the fifteenth century. New mathematical symbols were devised, some of which can be seen on the left of this print of 1491.

♦ LUCA PACIOLI
A Franciscan monk, Pacioli lived from 1445 to 1514. In 1487 he published his *Summa de aritmetica e geometria*, a popular work which greatly influenced his contemporaries. He was on friendly terms with Leonardo, teaching him the geometry of Euclid and Archimedes.

♦ MOVEABLE TYPE
The technique of printing with moveable type was perfected by Johannes Gutenberg in 1439. Invented by the Chinese three centuries earlier, the moveable characters were first made of terracotta or wood. Gutenberg had the brilliant idea of casting them in lead, which meant they could be made in far greater quantities and much reduced in size. This made printing quicker and cheaper.

THE GOLDEN SECTION ♦
Luca Pacioli published a work entitled *De divina proportione*. It was concerned with polygons and solids, and the proportional relationship later referred to as the golden section. The book was illustrated by Leonardo.

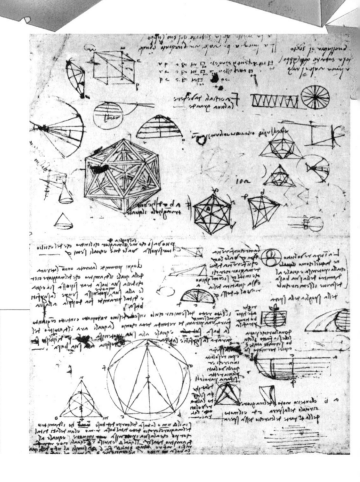

♦ POLYGONS
A page from Leonardo's notebook devoted to geometrical shapes. It contains a study for one of the polygons he drew for Luca Pacioli's *De divine proportione*.

♦ **VOYAGES OF DISCOVERY**
In 1492 Christopher Columbus made landfall in San Salvador. It was the start of a series of great ocean voyages. Traditional navigation systems proved inadequate, and sailors devised new methods of determining latitude and longitude.

♦ **CARTOGRAPHY**
Gerhard Kremer, known as Mercator (1495-1594), was one of the great cartographers of Leonardo's day. He revolutionized map-making by introducing the projection that bears his name. The Mercator projection is still in use today.

♦ **THE SANTA MARIA**
The caravel in which Columbus reached America.

ACCOUNTING ♦
Commercial practice required highly complex calculations. The instrument traditionally used was the abacus. Manuals on accounting were among the first printed books to gain a wide circulation.

♦ **PYTHAGORAS' THEOREM**
On this page of Leonardo's notebook, a diagram showing Pythagoras' theorem is found close to a preparatory drawing for *The Battle of Anghiari*.

☞ *Verrocchio died in Venice in 1488; Lorenzo the Magnificent, in Florence, in 1492. Meanwhile, in Milan, Leonardo jumped from one occupation to another. He acted as manager and stage designer for the magnificent court entertainments. In painting, he influenced a whole new trend. But it was science that most absorbed him: even art, in as much as it was founded on perfect imitation of nature, seemed to him to depend on scientific investigation. He had close ties with the mathematicians who came to Milan, in particular Luca Pacioli, to whom he showed his notes for his treatises on light, motion, explosions and weights. Pacioli calculated the volume of Leonardo's projected horse, and worked out how much bronze would be needed to cast the monument.* ☞

THE LAST SUPPER

This is the dramatic moment in the gospels when Christ, meeting with his disciples to celebrate the Jewish Passover, announces that one of them will betray him. Leonardo depicted the scene in a novel way. Instead of choosing the moment in which the identity of the traitor is revealed, he focuses on the reactions and gestures of the apostles as they question the Master: "Is it I, Lord?" Jesus sits impassive, while his disciples, all potential traitors, look questioningly at one another to protest their innocence.

♦ **THE WORK**
Tempera and oil on a plaster wall, 460 x 880 cm (15 x 29 feet). Santa Maria delle Grazie, Milan. Painted towards the end of Leonardo's first stay in Milan, between 1495 and

♦ **GROTESQUES**
Another aspect of Leonardo's interest in facial expressions is apparent in his grotesque portraits.

1498, the *Last Supper* was commissioned by Ludovico il Moro. It was done on the end wall of the monastery refectory, facing a representation of the *Crucifixion*. For technical reasons, the *Last Supper* soon began to deteriorate. It has been restored, retouched and repainted many times, but without great success. Recently it underwent delicate treatment to remove earlier over-paintings.

Why did the artist choose this particular moment for his painting of the Last Supper? Leonardo was a keen student of physiognomy, the science which seeks to establish a person's character from his or her features and facial expression. He observed that every emotion has its corresponding reaction or gesture, which differs with the age and character of the person concerned. By choosing this moment of self-questioning, Leonardo

was able to record varying reactions to a single stimulus. For instance, a preparatory drawing for the figure of James is shown top left. "Men's gestures are as varied as the thoughts running through their minds," Leonardo wrote. Observing the apostles, dramatically arranged in groups of three, we experience something of what they felt on the evening when Christ announced his supreme sacrifice.

♦ **THE FIRST IDEA**
Leonardo's intention to depict the moment at which Jesus announced his betrayal is evident in this preliminary drawing.

ANDREA DEL CASTAGNO
Painted in 1450 for the refectory of Santa Apollonia in Florence, Andrea del Castagno's *Last Supper* shows Judas Iscariot isolated on the near side of the table. Judas was traditionally shown from behind, separate from the other eleven, often reaching his hand into the dish with Jesus.

MATTHEW
Arms outstretched towards Jesus, Matthew addresses the two disciples at the end of the table. His face wears an expression of incredulity and desperation.

PHILIP
The gesture Leonardo used here was traditional: Philip draws his hands in to his chest, as in Ghirlandaio's painting.

ANDREW
His hands raised, palms towards the viewer, the apostle seems to be warding off something disagreeable.

JUDAS
In shadow, Judas is the only disciple not manifesting an emotional reaction. He alone shares the dramatic secret with Jesus.

GHIRLANDAIO
Domenico Ghirlandaio painted this version of the *Last Supper* for the Florentine convent of Ognissanti in 1480. As in the painting by Andrea del Castagno, the apostles are seated in a row on the far side of the table with Jesus, while Judas sits alone, opposite the man he is to betray.

Viewing the Painting

Throughout the Middle Ages the Last Supper was depicted as one part of the full cycle of Christ's passion, usually beginning with his entry into Jerusalem and ending with the entombment. Not until later, during the fifteenth century, was it chosen as an independent subject. It then became an important theme for paintings which were to cover a whole wall of a monastery refectory: the room where the monks met to eat their meals. The inner meaning of the Last Supper was lived on a daily basis by the monks and their prior. Like Jesus and the apostles, they sought to practise divine teaching by studying and conforming to the holy scriptures.

♦ The effects of bombing
This was the state of the refectory after the bombing raid of August 1943. The protective curtain prevented flying debris from causing irreparable damage.

♦ Technique
Always dissatisfied with his achievements, Leonardo took a very long time over his works, which is why so many are unfinished. If he had painted his mural of the Last Supper using the traditional fresco technique, he would have had to work very quickly: covering the area of plaster prepared for him each day while it was still damp. Because he knew he would want to rework parts of his painting, Leonardo adopted the technique of applying a mixture of oil and tempera over two layers of plaster. He could not have predicted that these materials would succumb to the attacks of pollution and humidity. During Leonardo's own lifetime an irreversible process of deterioration set in. The colours now are dull and neutral, but originally they were probably vivid and luminous. The heads of Jesus and Andrew (below) are shown.

If the spectator views the painting of the Last Supper *from a standpoint four metres (13 feet) off the ground (which was the height at which Leonardo worked), the scene appears to be an extension of the real architecture of the refectory. The vanishing point in fact coincides with Christ's head, the central feature of the composition (see the illustration on page 45). The remarkable thing is that the same sense of continuity between real space and picture space is also commmunicated to spectators at ground level. How did Leonardo achieve this effect? The diagram above shows that Leonardo constructed a kind of stage set. He "tipped" his painting towards the refectory to reveal the top of the table, and "forced" the perspective to increase the illusion of depth. For additional realism, he made it appear that the light was falling from the right, as if from the refectory's own windows.*

Still life ♦
The objects on the table are painted with the care normally devoted to a still life.

♦ A theatrical effect
The ideal standpoint from which to view the *Last Supper* is the place occupied by the prior at meal-times. Here, the spectator receives the full benefit of Leonardo's double perspective effect: the architecture in the painting appears as a continuation of the real refectory building; and the figure of Christ seems to offer the bread and wine from the picture to the real spectators outside.

WAR

Defensive systems were all-important in the Middle Ages. The heavy armour worn by horsemen offered protection against swords and arrows, and castle walls would resist the longest siege. In the fifteenth century the rules of war were revolutionized by the development of fire-arms: mounted knights and crossbowmen were replaced by soldiers with handguns and artillerymen, and the balance swung in favour of attack. In centres producing weapons, such as Milan, armour, swords, lances and halberds took second place to arquebus and cannon. Military architecture, too, underwent a transformation, and new defensive systems were developed. Walls became lower and thicker; towers were built with rounded contours to deflect cannon balls; fortifications were designed so that attackers could be kept constantly under fire.

♦ WAR: COLLECTIVE MADNESS
Leonardo described war as "bestial madness", but made many sketches for new military machines. In this he was not unlike some modern scientists who, while hating war, helped to manufacture the atomic bomb.

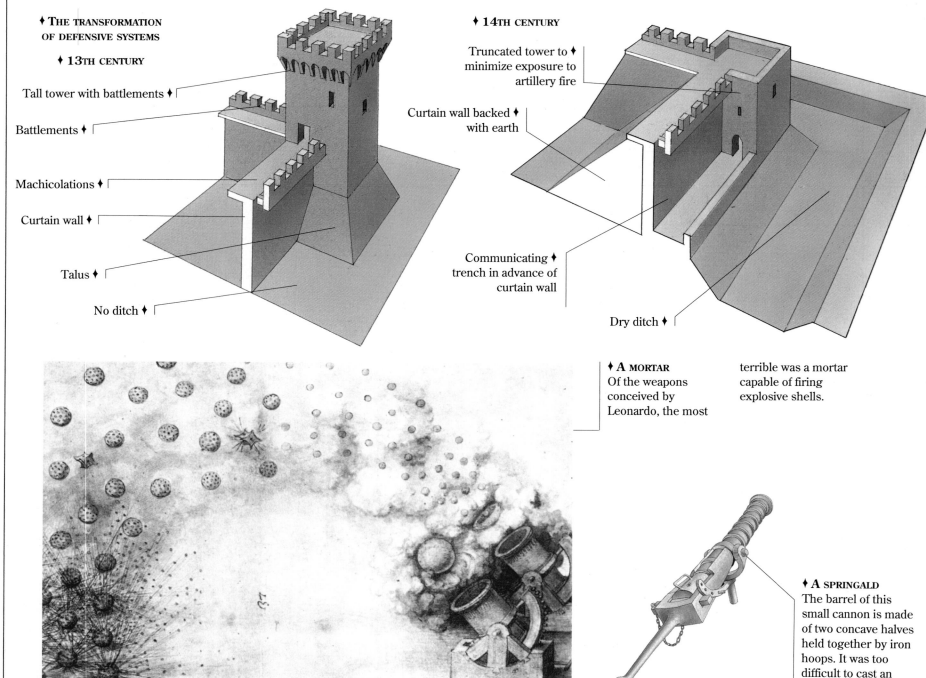

♦ THE TRANSFORMATION OF DEFENSIVE SYSTEMS

♦ 13TH CENTURY

Tall tower with battlements ♦

Battlements ♦

Machicolations ♦

Curtain wall ♦

Talus ♦

No ditch ♦

♦ 14TH CENTURY

Truncated tower to ♦ minimize exposure to artillery fire

Curtain wall backed ♦ with earth

Communicating ♦ trench in advance of curtain wall

Dry ditch ♦

♦ A MORTAR
Of the weapons conceived by Leonardo, the most terrible was a mortar capable of firing explosive shells.

♦ A SPRINGALD
The barrel of this small cannon is made of two concave halves held together by iron hoops. It was too difficult to cast an artillery piece whole.

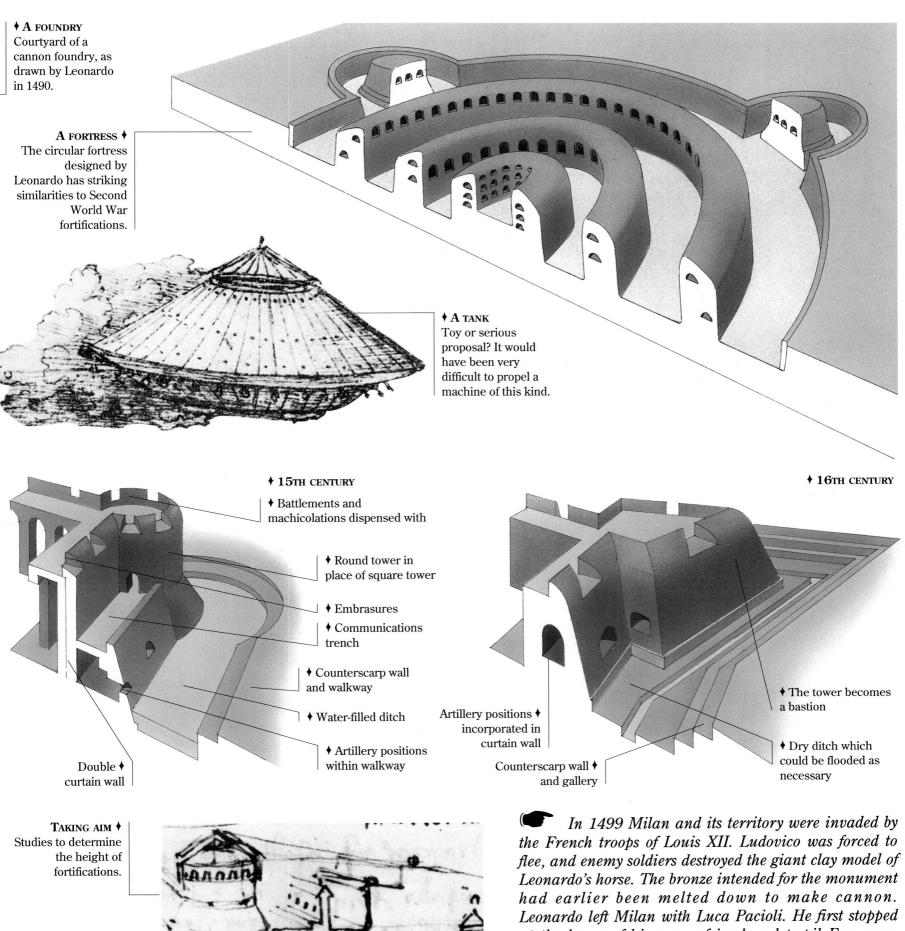

♦ A FOUNDRY
Courtyard of a cannon foundry, as drawn by Leonardo in 1490.

A FORTRESS ♦
The circular fortress designed by Leonardo has striking similarities to Second World War fortifications.

♦ A TANK
Toy or serious proposal? It would have been very difficult to propel a machine of this kind.

♦ 15TH CENTURY

♦ Battlements and machicolations dispensed with

♦ Round tower in place of square tower

♦ Embrasures

♦ Communications trench

♦ Counterscarp wall and walkway

♦ Water-filled ditch

♦ Artillery positions within walkway

Double ♦ curtain wall

♦ 16TH CENTURY

♦ The tower becomes a bastion

Artillery positions ♦ incorporated in curtain wall

Counterscarp wall ♦ and gallery

♦ Dry ditch which could be flooded as necessary

TAKING AIM ♦
Studies to determine the height of fortifications.

♦ A MACHINE GUN
The barrels are arranged in a fan to obtain a machine-gun effect.

☛ *In 1499 Milan and its territory were invaded by the French troops of Louis XII. Ludovico was forced to flee, and enemy soldiers destroyed the giant clay model of Leonardo's horse. The bronze intended for the monument had earlier been melted down to make cannon. Leonardo left Milan with Luca Pacioli. He first stopped at the home of his young friend and pupil Francesco Melzi at Vaprio. He then moved on to Mantua, where he made a charcoal drawing of Isabella d'Este. Fearing the arrival of the French, she urged Leonardo to depart, but later regretted her decision and in vain begged the artist to return. Leonardo went on to Venice and finally, in April 1500, returned to Florence. Since 1494, when the Medicis had been expelled, the city had experienced a period of republican government. Leonardo was offered hospitality in the Servite convent of the Santissima Annunziata. There he displayed the cartoon for a painting of the* Virgin and Child with St Anne, *which greatly impressed the Florentines.* ☛

RIVALRY WITH MICHELANGELO

In 1497 the republican government of Florence enlarged the ancient seat of government – known as the Palazzo Vecchio – by adding a council chamber capable of seating five hundred. Following the expulsion of the Medicis, the Florentine authorities, mindful of their prestige, commissioned many works of painting, sculpture and intarsia (mosaic woodwork). To decorate the walls of the new chamber, they chose the most famous contemporary artists: Leonardo and Michelangelo, who were fierce rivals. Their task was to depict two famous victories won by Florentine armies. Unfortunately, little survives of their efforts. Michelangelo drew the cartoons for his *Battle of Cascina*, but they have since been lost. For his painting, the *Battle of Anghiari*, Leonardo wanted to revive a mural technique used by the Romans: encaustic. The results were disappointing. The colours ran, spoiling the whole work.

♦ THE FLORENTINE REPUBLIC
The Medicis were expelled from Florence in 1494, and the city adopted a republican form of government. Niccolò Machiavelli, Michelangelo and Leonardo returned to live there, and Piero Soderini was elected *gonfaloniere*, or head

of state, in 1502. In those years the city was shaken by a Dominican monk, Girolamo Savonarola, who preached extreme puritanism. In 1498, Savonarola fell and was burned alive in the Piazza della Signoria. But the republic was short-lived, and soon the Medicis returned to power.

♦ ENCAUSTIC
Encaustic, developed around the fourth century BC, was the most widespread painting technique in the classical world. The pigments were mixed with hot wax before being applied.

Leonardo hoped to achieve a high-gloss effect. Unfortunately, he misinterpreted the instructions he had found in ancient texts. When he used braziers to heat the wall, the colours merged and ran.

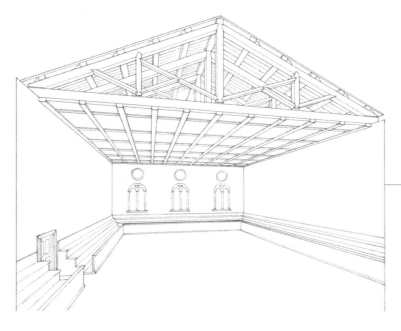

♦ THE COUNCIL CHAMBER
The council chamber as it appeared at the time. Leonardo was allocated the right-hand wall for the *Battle of Anghiari*.

♦ THE COUNCIL CHAMBER TODAY
Despite recent investigations, no trace of Leonardo's work has been found.

☛ *In 1502 Leonardo left Florence again and entered the service of Cesare Borgia, an ambitious military commander protected by his father, pope Alexander VI. With Cesare, Leonardo spent two years in the field, engaged on fortifications in the area between Urbino and the Adriatic coast. On his return to Florence, in 1503, he began his most famous painting, the* Mona Lisa. *There was sad news in 1504: his father had died, aged eighty, and Leonardo subsequently experienced great difficulty in obtaining his share of the inheritance. Meanwhile, he had to take up the challenge with Michelangelo. The cartoons for the* Battle of Anghiari *were to be completed by February 1505. He worked in the great council chamber, using the long-forgotten encaustic technique, but the results were disappointing and, embittered by his failure, Leonardo gave up the attempt.* ☛

♦A FAMOUS COPY
The Flemish painter
Peter Paul Rubens
(1577-1640) made a
copy of the central
scene of Leonardo's
Battle of Anghiari.

**PRELIMINARY ♦
DRAWINGS**
We can get some idea
of Leonardo's
intentions for the
Battle of Anghiari,
from the fine
drawings that
survive. The heads of
the warriors and
rearing horses
belong to the central
scene of the painting,
a ferocious struggle
for the standard
between Florentine
and Milanese
horsemen. The battle
was fought in 1440,
near the town of
Arezzo.

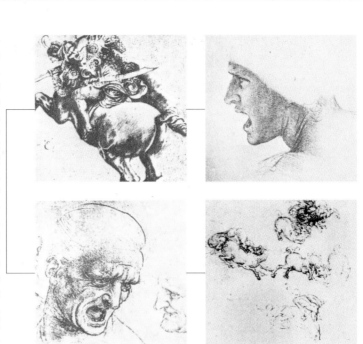

**♦A WORKING
PLATFORM**
An innovator in every
field, Leonardo
designed a working
platform that
captured the
imagination of his
contemporaries. By
turning a screw, the
workmen could raise
or lower the platform
to the required
height.

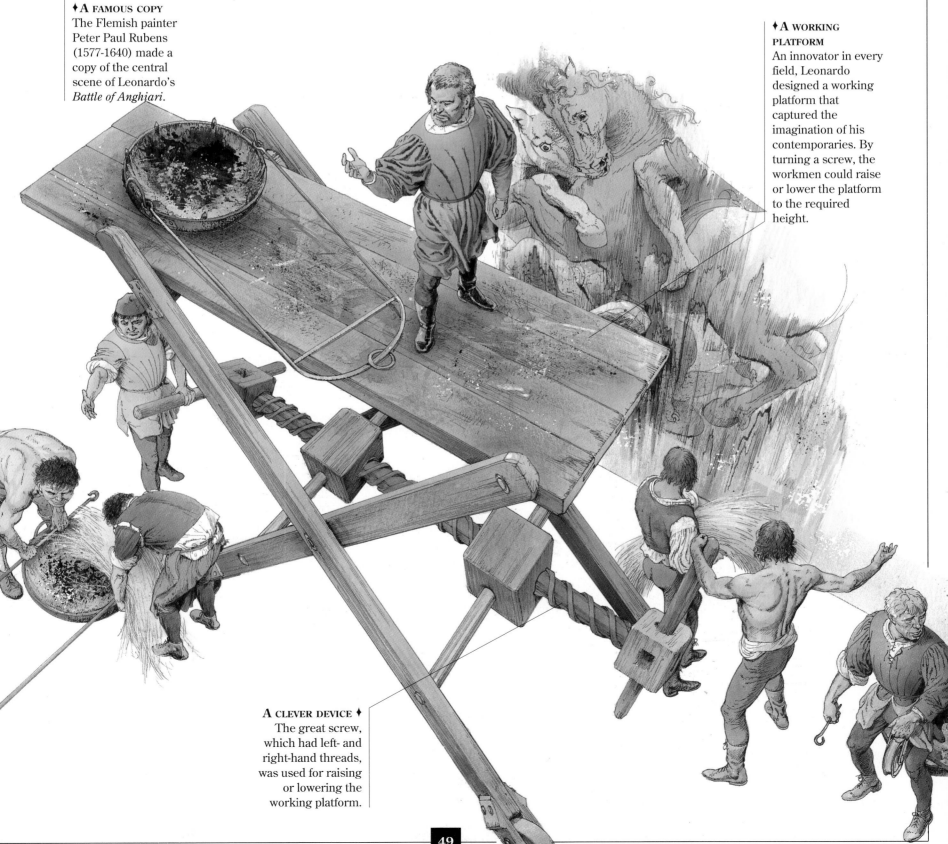

A CLEVER DEVICE ♦
The great screw,
which had left- and
right-hand threads,
was used for raising
or lowering the
working platform.

THE MONA LISA

The world's most famous painting is shrouded in mystery. But it is of no great importance whether the subject of the portrait is "Monna Lisa", wife of Florentine banker Francesco del Giocondo, or a favourite courtesan of Giuliano de' Medici. The lady with the enigmatic smile and intense gaze is depicted in a loggia. At her back is a magical, dream-like landscape of rocks and water.

♦ THE WORK
Oil on wooden panel, 77 x 53 cm (30 x 21 inches). Louvre, Paris. Shortly after his return to Florence in 1503, Leonardo began work on a portrait that was to occupy him, off and on, for the rest of his life. The unfinished painting followed him to Milan, Rome and finally France. Antonio De Beatis mentions seeing it when he visited Leonardo at Cloux in 1517. The painting passed through many hands, until finally Napoleon assigned it to the Louvre in 1805. Stolen in 1911 and brought back to Italy, it was exhibited in Florence, Rome and Milan before its final return to France. So subtle was Leonardo's technique that his brushstrokes are invisible, even when the painting is examined under X-rays. The work must have required infinite patience. The Mona Lisa has always been an object of curiosity. Imaginative artists have portrayed the lady in the most unusual guises. She is shown as nude in one seventeenth-century copy (above) and, in modern times, Salvador Dalì painted her with a moustache.

EARLY EXPERIMENTS ♦
In this early drawing of the countryside around his native village of Vinci (see page 7), Leonardo's interest in views from above is already evident.

♦ A STORM
This study of a deluge reveals Leonardo's interest in

atmospheric phenomena, and their effects on the quality of light.

Leonardo used "aerial" perspective in composing the landscape behind the Mona Lisa. That is, the further away things are, the more colours fade and lines become blurred. This gives a sense of depth. The *landscape has a magical atmosphere, with the bridge on the right the only sign of human existence. A different perspective is used for the figure, with her steady gaze and expressive mouth.*

MOUNTAIN RANGES ♦
In this preparatory drawing for the *Virgin and Child with St Anne*, we seem to view these mountain peaks from an aeroplane - a standpoint favoured by Leonardo.

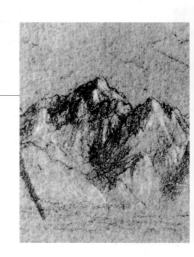

MOUNTAINS ✦
In this Madonna from 1480 - Alte Pinakothek, Munich - the quality of the atmosphere creates the sense of distance between the viewer and the mountains in the background.

✦ WATER
Leonardo was fascinated by the phenomenon of evaporation. In his misty landscapes, water and mountains appear to merge into each other.

✦ PERSPECTIVE
The landscape fades away into the muted blues and greens of the horizon. This effect is a result of the refraction of light in the atmosphere.

✦ AIR IS BLUE
Leonardo maintained that air is blue. The more distant an object, the more air between it and the observer: hence objects in the far distance take on a blue appearance.

LOOKING INTO ✦
THE DISTANCE
In Leonardo's *Bacchus* of 1515 - Louvre, Paris - the outlines of objects in the background soften with distance, until finally they merge into their surroundings.

Hydraulics

In Leonardo's day waterways were far more important than they are today. It was quicker and cheaper to transport goods by boat, because of the poor state of the roads and the inefficiency of existing vehicles. Canals were also useful for irrigation, and, where there was a fall in level, water power could be harnessed to drive grinding and fulling mills. Lying inland, Florence would benefit from an effective link with the sea, and for over a century the Florentines had dreamed of building a waterway to the Tyrrhenian Sea. The Arno ran dry in summer, and even in winter navigation was difficult because of the river's winding, irregular course. On his return to Florence, Leonardo studied how to build a navigable canal which would rejoin the Arno near Pisa, an ancient sea-going republic and rival of Florence. In considering this plan, Leonardo could draw on the wealth of experience he had acquired in Milan. There he had carried out many projects to improve Lombardy's canal network.

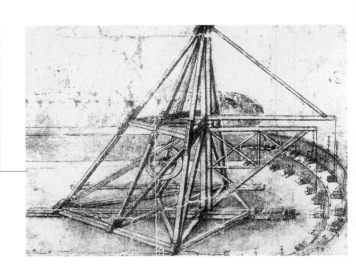

MACHINES, NOT MEN ♦
Realizing that men equipped only with spades and shovels would take years to complete so vast a project as diverting the Arno, Leonardo designed great excavating machines to hasten progress.

MOTIVE POWER ♦
Barges were towed along the canal by men and horses.

FILLING THE LOCK ♦
The sluices are opened, the lock fills with water, and the barge rises to the higher level.

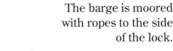

MOORING ♦
The barge is moored with ropes to the side of the lock.

ENTERING A LOCK ♦
The gates are open, and a barge travelling upstream enters the lock.

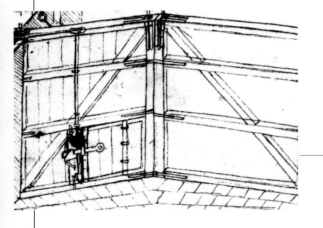

♦ **THE INVENTOR**
Leonardo is credited with the invention of many hydraulic devices, in particular the lock. Locks make it possible to control the water level in a confined section of canal, and so raise and lower boats from one level to another.

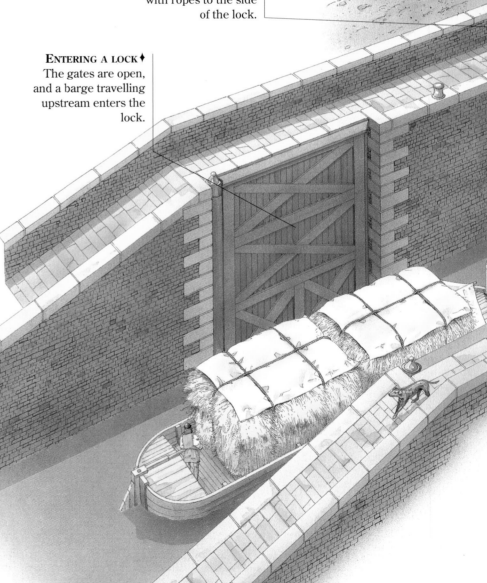

☞ *In 1503 Florence embarked on a debilitating war against her neighbour, Pisa. Niccolò Machiavelli, Florentine minister of war, had for some time been thinking of diverting the Arno, which runs through both cities, as a way of damaging Pisa's livelihood. Leonardo studied the problem and drew up a well-illustrated report. According to an old tradition, he was actually commissioned to begin the work, but this is improbable: to divert the river would have taken two thousand labourers forty thousand working days. The task was beyond Florence's means, and would have taken years to complete. In fact, the war ended in 1509. Leonardo's notes nevertheless demonstrate his ability in problem-solving.* ☞

THE CANAL ✦
The Arno, with its seasonal flow, was difficult to navigate. Leonardo planned a canal fed by the streams descending from the Apennines. The canal would have begun in Florence and rejoined the Arno near Pisa.

✦ THE TUNNEL
It would have been necessary to drive a tunnel one kilometre (1091 yards) long under the hill of Serravalle.

HOW A LOCK WORKS ✦
1. The sluices are opened and water fills the lock.
2. The lock is full.
3. The exit gate is opened and the boat continues its journey.

CANAL BRIDGE ✦
Canals often had to cross rivers.

SAINT ANNE

Seated on the knees of Saint Anne, Mary is depicted lifting the baby Jesus, who in turn is attempting to sit astride a struggling lamb. As she watches the child at play, Saint Anne - the mother of Mary - contemplates the miracle of the incarnation. The theme of the three generations was common in northern Europe, and eventually became popular with Italian painters, particularly in Florence.

♦ THE WORK
Oil on wooden panel, 168 x 130 cm (5.5 x 4.25 feet). Louvre, Paris. The *Virgin and Child with St Anne* is the final version of a subject on which Leonardo had been working for some time. He had already produced two cartoons and, possibly, an earlier painting. Leonardo painted the panel towards the end of his second stay in Milan, between 1510 and 1513. It accompanied him to France, together with the *Mona Lisa* and

St John the Baptist. He kept the three paintings by him until his death. Francesco Melzi, the pupil who inherited his works, brought the *St Anne* back to Italy, but in 1629 cardinal Richelieu, minister of Louis XIII, purchased it and took it to France as a gift for his sovereign. In 1801 it was added to the Louvre collections.

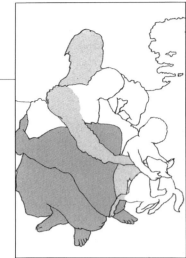

FORM ♦
The figures merge and it is difficult to say where one begins and another ends: Mary's arm could belong to Saint Anne, their legs are intertwined, and the Child's thigh is continued in the leg of the lamb.

♦ MOVEMENT
The figures are as if bound up together in a single movement: the Child is trying to grasp the lamb, while Mary restrains him, watched by Saint Anne. The group

tends towards the right-hand side of the picture, where their eyes also seem to converge on a single point. The observer is left with an acute sense of instability.

Leonardo treated the subject in a completely new way: in terms of composition, and of the interpretation he seems to be suggesting. The figures are as if interwoven, forming a compact mass *with the structure of a pyramid. Leonardo had already used this arrangement, but here he gives the group a dynamic sense of movement. Three preparatory drawings are shown on the left.*

COLOUR ♦
Warm and cold tones are perfectly balanced, creating a magical equilibrium of predominantly blue and brown tones.

♦ **A SYMBOL OF CHRIST'S PASSION**
In the religious ceremonies of the Old Testament, an animal offered in sacrifice had to be without spot or blemish. For Christians, the lamb became the symbol of Christ's sacrifice on the cross. By showing the infant Jesus embracing the creature, Leonardo suggests the purpose for which Christ came: innocent as a lamb, he was born to give his life as a sacrifice.

♦ **THE VIRGIN**
The Virgin Mary leans forward with all the solicitude of a mother wanting to protect her baby. By this simple, gentle gesture, Leonardo represents the instinct of a mother seeking to avert the tragic destiny awaiting her child.

MASOLINO AND ♦ MASACCIO, 1420
In this static, pyramid-shaped arrangement, Saint Anne is depicted as an old woman, solemnly dominating the composition.

♦ **FIRST THOUGHTS**
In the 1498 cartoon in the National Gallery, London, the allusion is more explicit: Saint Anne points upwards to indicate that this is God's will.

♦ **SAINT ANNE**
Supporting the whole group, the dignified figure of Saint Anne looks on with an expression of sweet resignation. For Leonardo, she represents the Church. The primeval landscape in the background suggests the passage of time: Saint Anne knows that Christ's sacrifice is inevitable, and feels pity for her daughter.

FLIGHT

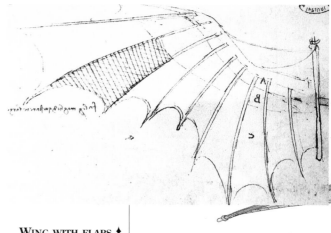

Strangely enough, it is Leonardo's most fantastic project - his attempt to create a flying machine - that best demonstrates the way his mind worked. He began by observing birds, studying the anatomy of their wings, and the function and arrangement of their feathers. Watching them in flight, he noted that the wing-beat was different for take-off, forward flight and landing. His first idea was that a man might fly by flapping a large pair of wings, but he soon realized that human muscle power was insufficient. He next considered a mechanical propulsion system worked by a spring, but it was apparent that the spring would unwind too quickly for sustained flight. He therefore returned to his study of birds, observing how large raptors are borne up by air currents. He took into account the importance of atmospheric conditions: wind speed and direction, and meteorological and aerodynamic factors. Finally, he concluded that, in the absence of an engine - not invented until centuries later - the best prospect for human flight lay in fixed-wing gliding. He then designed a machine similar to a modern hang-glider.

♦ THE WING-BEAT OF BIRDS
Leonardo started by studying the way birds beat their wings.

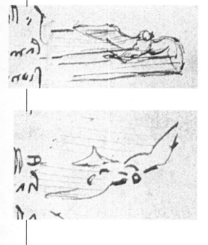

WING WITH FLAPS ♦
Leonardo observed that, when birds come in to land, their feathers are held tightly together. From this he wrongly deduced that birds in normal flight spread their feathers to allow air to pass through. And so he designed a wing with flaps that would open on take-off and close on landing.

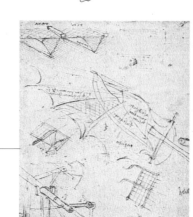

A FLYING MACHINE ♦
The wings were worked by the hands and feet of the pilot.

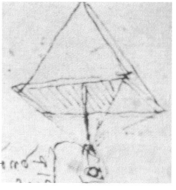

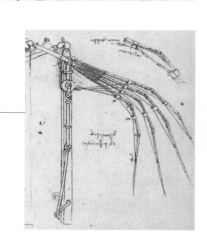

FUTURE INVENTIONS ♦
Leonardo anticipated the helicopter and the parachute.

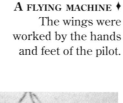

SPRING-DRIVEN ♦
Leonardo designed spring-driven wings which would flap up and down like those of a bird.

♦ HOW BIRDS FLY
Finding it impossible to design wings light enough to be worked by human muscle power, Leonardo turned his attention to the gliding flight of birds.

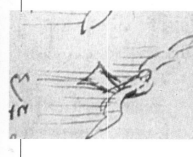

FIXED WING ♦
A fixed wing, with appendages to control the machine. Leonardo had adopted the principle of the hang-glider.

☞ *In 1506 Leonardo abandoned his work on the council chamber and returned to Milan, where the French were now in power. Charles of Amboise, the governor, invited him to stay and promised commissions, possibly even a portrait of the French king, Louis XII. Apart from a brief journey to Florence, in 1508, Leonardo again made his home in Milan, enthusiastically pursuing his scientific interests. He made geological and hydrographical studies of the Lombard valleys, continued work on his* Virgin and Child with St Anne, *and tackled difficult problems of geometry. He received a regular allowance from the king of France, but was embittered by a law-suit with his brothers over their father's estate. In 1512 the Sforzas were restored to power in Milan. The following year Leonardo and some of his companions, Francesco Melzi included, left the city for good and made their way to Rome.* ☞

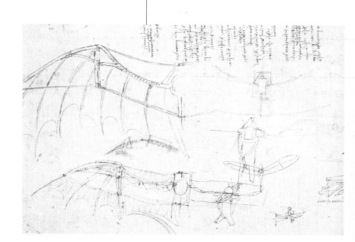

♦ INTEGRAL WING
After experimenting with opening flaps, Leonardo opted for an integral wing, similar to the wing of a bat.

IMPROVEMENTS ♦
Leonardo tried out other materials and improved the framework. He was moving towards the concept of gliding.

Mechanics

Leonardo's interest in mechanical engineering is amply proved by the thousands of his drawings that remain. When these were first published, a hundred or so years ago, they created a sensation, and many people saw Leonardo as having anticipated almost all modern inventions, from the helicopter to the bicycle. We are now more aware of his debt to earlier inventors, and to his contemporaries: many of the machines he drew had already been built, or at least existed in the minds of imaginative engineers. Leonardo was original in having understood that the working of any machine, be it a crane or a water-mill, depends on a limited number of mechanisms: springs, connecting rods, cams, gears, and so on. The way to obtain better machines was therefore to study and improve their component parts.

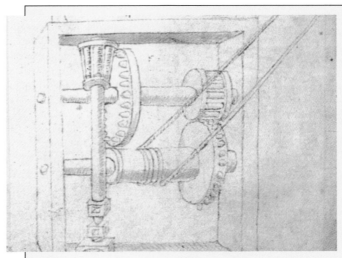

♦A LIFTING MACHINE
A drawing of a type of winch, by Francesco di Giorgio, architect, engineer and friend of Leonardo. It gives a general idea of the winch and its gearing system. Compared with this, Leonardo's drawings were more detailed and explored how machines worked.

♦LEONARDO'S DRAWINGS
On page 59 are study drawings by Leonardo of different mechanisms. The drawing on this page is one he made of another kind of winch for lifting things. On the left he shows what the machine looks like. Then, on the right, he gives an exploded version in an attempt to explain how the machine works.

♦RATCHET WHEEL
The pawl on the drum would catch the teeth on the inside of the ratchet wheel and so make it turn.

♦LEVER
Moving the lever back and forth would make first one, then the other of the ratchet wheels turn.

♦LOAD
The weight to be lifted would be attached to the rope, which was wound round the shaft.

SHAFT ♦
Made to turn by the wheels, the shaft would wind in the rope.

In 1513 Leonardo arrived in Rome, where he was a guest of the Florentine cardinal Giuliano de' Medici, brother of the new pope Leo X. The greatest artists of the day had gravitated to Rome. Bramante died there in 1514, and Raphael took over the responsibility for building St Peter's. Leonardo was not obliged to paint, but designed the stage sets for some of the lavish Roman entertainments. He continued his scientific studies, particularly mathematics, studying the problem of squaring the circle and beginning a treatise on geometry. In 1514 or 1515 Leo X gave him the task of draining the swampy, unhealthy countryside around Rome - a project to which he devoted two years. Louis XII of France died in 1515 and his successor, Francis I, offered Leonardo hospitality at the French court. After one more year in Rome, in 1517 Leonardo set off for France, where he was to live out the rest of his life.

CAM ♦
A cam transfers the movement of a rotating shaft to another part of the machine. In some internal combustion engines, cams open and close the valves.

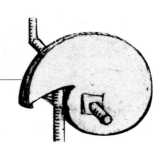

COUPLING ♦
Leonardo designed many kinds of coupling. Their purpose is to connect two mechanical parts.

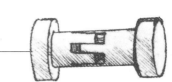

♦ DRUM
Each half of the double drum has a pawl, which would engage with the ratchet teeth in one direction only. As each wheel rotated, the dowels would turn the shaft, lifting the load.

♦ OPPOSING RATCHET WHEEL
This wheel would rotate in the opposite direction to its partner.

PULLEY ♦
A pulley is a wheel with a rope or belt on its rim. Pulleys can be used for lifting weights and for transmitting power.

CHAIN ♦
Drive chains are used to transmit power from one part of a machine to another. The most obvious example is a bicycle chain.

CLUTCH ♦
A clutch, consisting of two parts which can be connected and disconnected, is used to engage and disengage a mechanism.

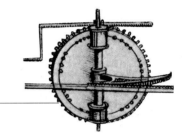

COG-WHEELS ♦
Cogs are vital components. They transmit power from one shaft to another and, depending on their size, increase or decrease the speed of rotation.

BEARINGS ♦
Leonardo designed many kinds of ball and roller bearing, to reduce friction.

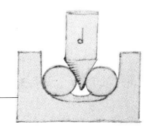

WORM ♦
Leonardo called the worm of a helical gear a "perpetual screw". This type of gear transmits power between shafts at right angles to each other, and permits large reductions in rotational speeds.

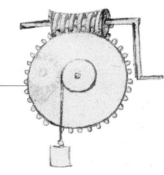

ESCAPEMENT ♦
A device which regulates the motion of rotating mechanisms, used most often in clocks.

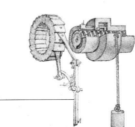

TEETH AND DOWELS ♦
A close-up of the teeth and dowels of the ratchet wheel.

SCREW ♦
A screw combining a right-hand and a left-hand thread doubles the speed of a mechanism.

FRANCE

Leonardo's story ends in France, at the court of Francis I, where even in the last months of his life he engaged in one of his favourite activities: designing the sets and machinery for lavish entertainments. When he died at Cloux, not yet seventy years of age, honoured by king and courtiers alike, his legacy to posterity was immense. Leonardo was one of the greatest painters of all time, a sculptor, a brilliant engineer, architect, scientist and musician. More than that, his extraordinary gifts, never before combined in a single person, laid the foundation for a new vision of man and his environment. Leonardo was the first "modern human". His questing mind was never satisfied, but sought always to probe further into the unknown, to overcome the restrictions of fixed modes of thought and behaviour and extend the frontiers of human knowledge.

✦ **LEONARDO'S DEATH**
This famous drawing by the French painter Dominique Ingres (1780-1867) depicts Leonardo's death. Although Francis I is shown at the bedside, the king was not in fact present during his last moments. It is true, however, that he was devoted to Leonardo.

✦ **ROBOTS**
Leonardo had a passion for automata. To mark a celebration in honour of Francis, he constructed a mechanical lion. At the crucial moment the lion opened to eject its load of white lilies, symbol of the French crown.

♦ AMBOISE
Leonardo spent the last years of his life close to the royal residence of Amboise at Cloux.

REMORANTIN ♦
A plan for the château of Remorantin, which Leonardo undertook for Francis's wife. It was never built.

ST JOHN ♦
This *St John the Baptist* - executed after 1510 and now in the Louvre - was Leonardo's last known painting. The artist brought it with him to France, and bequeathed it to his friend and pupil Francesco Melzi.

♦ MELZI
Francesco Melzi, Leonardo's favourite pupil and assistant, watches the reaction to Leonardo's contrivance.

♦ WHAT LEONARDO LOOKED LIKE
Above: the figure of Plato in Raphael's *School of Athens* (Vatican), thought to be a portrait of Leonardo. Left: a supposed self-portrait, drawn by Leonardo in 1512. The artist looks older than his years.

♦ CHAMBORD
The château de Chambord. There is no definite evidence, but Leonardo may have influenced its design.

☞ *Francis I was well aware of Leonardo's genius, and heaped honours upon him. He gave him a princely residence at Cloux, near Amboise; granted him a pension; and bestowed on him the title of first painter, architect and mechanic of the King. Despite losing the use of one arm, Leonardo showed that his appetite for work was undiminished. For a celebration to honour the king, he built a mechanical lion; he helped organize other royal festivities; and he produced studies for irrigation projects in various French cities. In 1519 his health took a turn for the worse. In April he made his will, leaving all his manuscripts to Francesco Melzi. He died on 2 May. Legend has it that Francis I, who admired him greatly and regarded him almost as a father, hurried to his bedside at Amboise to pay his last respects.*

◆ KEY DATES

1452 Leonardo born at Vinci on 15 April, natural child of ser Piero, a notary, and Caterina, a peasant girl in service with the family.

1469 Joins the workshop of Andrea del Verrocchio, in Florence, where he learns the techniques of drawing, painting and sculpture.

1473 Now a member of the painters' guild of St Luke. Executes the first work that can be ascribed to him with certainty: a drawing of the Arno valley.

1478 Paints an altarpiece for the Palazzo della Signoria, Florence. Failure of the Pazzi conspiracy against the Medicis; Lorenzo de' Medici's authority confirmed.

1482 Moves to Milan, where he is commissioned to create a colossal equestrian statue in memory of Francesco Sforza, and employs his talents in many other fields.

1492 Designs costumes for the wedding of Ludovico il Moro and Beatrice d'Este. Death of Lorenzo the Magnificent. Columbus sails to the New World.

1495 Begins painting the *Last Supper* in the refectory of Santa Maria delle Grazie, a monastery in Milan. Decorates parts of the Sforza castle.

1499 Leaves Milan with the mathematician Luca Pacioli. Stays at Vaprio, then Mantua, where he makes two portraits of Isabella d'Este.

1500 In March, returns from Venice to Florence, where he lodges at the Servite convent of the Santissima Annunziata.

1502 Serves Cesare Borgia as architect and engineer during military campaigns in the Romagna region. Studies fortification systems and war machines.

1503 Back in Florence, paints the *Mona Lisa*. The Florentine Republic commissions him to paint the *Battle of Anghiari* in the Palazzo Vecchio.

1504 Works on the *Battle of Anghiari*. Michelangelo completes his *David*. Raphael moves to Florence, and is deeply influenced by Leonardo's work.

1508 Returns to Milan and devotes himself to geology and anatomy. In Rome, Michelangelo is commissioned to paint the Sistine ceiling.

1513 Leaves for Rome, where he spends three years in the service of the Medici pope Leo X. Pursues mathematical and scientific studies.

1514 Draws up plans for draining the Pontine marshes. Death of Bramante; Raphael succeeds him as architect of St Peter's.

1517 Francis I, the new king of France, having reconquered Milan, invites Leonardo to his court. Leonardo takes up residence at Cloux, near Amboise.

1518 Designs the stage sets for the wedding of Lorenzo de' Medici and a niece of the French king. Takes part in celebrations for the Dauphin's baptism.

1519 Charles V elected Holy Roman Emperor. A sick man, Leonardo makes his will on 23 April, naming his painter friend Francesco Melzi as executor. Dies at Cloux on 2 May.

◆ LEONARDO'S NOTEBOOKS

Right up to the end of his life Leonardo continued his scientific studies and made prodigious quantities of notes. Several times he attempted to set them in order, but none of the books he embarked on was ever finished, and his observations remained fragmentary, unconnected and at times contradictory. On Leonardo's death, this priceless collection of writings, many of them illustrated with drawings and sketches, passed to Francesco Melzi, who began to catalogue them. The work was extremely difficult: Leonardo's notes were usually very short, and often intended only for his own use. He sometimes repeated himself in different places, copied extracts from other writers' works and, years later, would fill in empty spaces in earlier manuscripts. His notes were not always dated. Reordering his writings on a chronological basis was clearly very difficult. Melzi nevertheless managed to reorganize at least part of the material in a logical way and, following the master's original intentions, compiled the *Treatise on Painting*, which now constitutes the Vatican Library's CODEX URBINAS. When Melzi died, in 1570, the manuscripts went various ways, and some were lost, dismembered or mutilated. Roughly 3500 pages have survived, mostly written on both sides of the paper and illustrated with drawings. Some are in the form of small note-pads, which Leonardo used for making rapid observations. There are also more substantial exercise books intended for specific studies, but which generally degenerated into collections of heterogeneous notes, and a large number of loose sheets. Most are written in an apparently indecipherable hand, which some of Leonardo's contemporaries took to be a form of secret code. It is in fact mirror writing: the artist wrote from right to left using his left hand.

THE "ATLANTIC" AND WINDSOR CODICES. Some decades after Melzi's death, the Milanese Pompeo Leoni, official sculptor to king Philip II of Spain and art collector, tried to reassemble some of the scattered manuscripts. He catalogued and numbered a good part of Leonardo's writings and a large number of individual sheets, and collected them into two substantial volumes. The first, kept in the library of Windsor Castle, is a compilation of some six hundred drawings, including studies for drapery and for the *Last Supper*. It also contains a plan of the town of Imola – the first such survey carried out on scientific lines – and almost all Leonardo's anatomical studies. The second volume, kept in the Ambrosian Library in Milan and universally known as the "Atlantic" Codex, possibly on account of its size (in Greek mythology, Atlas was the giant who supported the world on his shoulders), contains drawings and writings on scientific subjects. It includes notes on artillery and on offensive and defensive weapons, plans for a self-propelled carriage (still referred to as "Leonardo's automobile") and early drawings for a flying machine. There is also a curious sketch of a bicycle, surprisingly like modern versions, drawn on the reverse of one of Leonardo's sheets by a pupil, who was copying an original by the artist, now lost.

MANUSCRIPTS A-M AND ASHBURNHAM CODEX. In 1635 the Atlantic Codex found its way to the Ambrosian Library in Milan, together with twelve other manuscripts identified by the letters A to M. In 1796 Napoleon decreed that all these volumes be expropriated and sent to the library of the Institut de France in Paris. Only the Atlantic Codex was eventually returned. The oldest of all these compilations is manuscript B, dating from 1488, which contains drawings of war machines, boats, bridges and flying machines. 1490 and 1491 are covered by manuscripts C and A respectively, the latter devoted largely to painting and physics. A part of Manuscript A today forms the separate codex known as Ashburnham, on painting. Manuscripts H and I, which also belong to Leonardo's first Milanese period, are concerned with grammar and lexicology. The others – D, E, F, G, K, L and M – are devoted to scientific topics.

THE TRIVULZIANO CODEX. This is one of the oldest collections of Leonardo's writings, dating from his early years in Milan. Kept in the Castello Sforzesco, it contains notes on grammar and lexicology, and long lists of words, mainly deriving from Latin. Leonardo had not received much formal education, but knowledge of Latin was indispensable for reading most scientific texts. This codex bears witness to his desire to master it.

THE FORSTER MANUSCRIPTS. Three small notebooks, kept at the Victoria and Albert Museum, London. The most important, Forster I, consists of fifteen pages, dating from 1490, sewn into a bigger notebook compiled in 1505. It contains diagrams of hydraulic devices, demonstrating Leonardo's fascination with the world of water. The other two are devoted to Euclidian geometry, which Leonardo learned from his friend Luca Pacioli.

MADRID I AND MADRID II. Not discovered until the 1960s, these two codices, inventory numbers 8937 and 8936, are kept in the National Library, Madrid. The first, begun during Leonardo's early years in Milan, contains illustrations of machinery, particularly for textile manufacture, and mechanical components (screws, chains, cogs, pulleys, fly-wheels, ball bearings, gears, clock parts). The second includes a report on the problems of casting his bronze horse, the project for diverting the waters of the Arno, and plans for the fortification of Piombino.

HAMMER (FORMERLY LEICESTER) CODEX. The writings and many of the drawings in this codex are concerned with a topic of special fascination to Leonardo: water and its dynamics: flow, currents, whirlpools, rapids. There is also material on astronomy and geology, with theories about the structure of the earth and the way its surface changes.

CODEX ON BIRD FLIGHT. Kept in the Biblioteca Reale in Turin, this collection was compiled around 1505 and contains studies and drawings of birds, their anatomy and their mode of flight in different atmospheric conditions. There are also pages devoted to quite different subjects, in particular mechanics, hydraulics and architecture.

ARUNDEL MANUSCRIPT. Kept at the British Museum, this is a compilation of notebooks on various subjects recorded by Leonardo in the final decades of his life. In his treatment of water, he returns to the theme of the Hammer Codex and the drawings of *The Deluge* owned by Queen Elizabeth II. Leonardo planned to enlarge on this subject in a work entitled *Libro primo delle acque*.

♦ LIST OF WORKS INCLUDED IN THIS BOOK

The works reproduced in this book are listed here, with their date, when known, the museum or gallery where they are now held, and page number. The numbers in bold type refer to the Credits on page 64, which give further information about some of the works. Where no gallery is shown, the work is in a private collection. Abbreviations: Atlantic Codex, AC; Arundel Codex, ARC; Windsor Codex, WC; codex on bird flight, BFC; Madrid I, MI; Madrid II, MII; Manuscript B, MB; Manuscript L, ML.

ANONYMOUS
1 *Nude Mona Lisa*, 17th century (Kaupe collection, Pallanza) 50.
ANDREA DEL CASTAGNO (c.1421-1457)
2 *Last Supper*, 1450 (refectory of the convent of Santa Apollonia, Florence) 43.
APOLLONIO DI GIOVANNI (c.1415-1465)
3 *Banquet in a Courtyard*, c.1460 (Biblioteca Riccardiana, Florence) 29.
BELLINI, GIOVANNI (c.1432-1516)
4 *Pietà*, c.1460 (Museo Correr, Venice) 16.
BOTTICELLI, SANDRO (1445-1510)
5 *Adoration of the Magi*, 1480 (Uffizi Gallery, Florence) 27; **6** *Annunciation*, c.1470 (Louis F. Hyde collection, Glen Falls, New York) 18; **7** *Birth of Venus*, 1482 (Uffizi Gallery, Florence) 16; **8** *Head of Angel*, c.1480 (Musée des Beaux-Arts, Rennes) 15.
BRUNELLESCHI, FILIPPO (1377-1446)
9 *Crucifix*, c.1410-15 (Gondi chapel, church of Santa Maria Novella, Florence) 10; **10** *Sacrifice of Isaac*, bronze panel for door of Florence Baptistry, 1401 (Bargello Museum, Florence) 10.
DALI, SALVADOR (1904-1979)
11 *Mona Lisa with Moustache*, 50.
DOMENICO VENEZIANO (byname of Domenico di Bartolomeo) (early 15th century-1461)
12 *Annunciation*, 1445-48 (Fitzwilliam Museum, Cambridge, England) 19.
DONATELLO (byname of Niccolò di Betto Bardi) (1386-1466)
13 *Crucifix*, c. 1410-15 (church of Santa Croce, Florence) 10; **14** *The Feast of Herod*, 1427 (cathedral baptistry, Siena) 11; **15** *Equestrian statue of Gattamelata*, c. 1446-50 (Piazza del Santo, Padua) 31.
GHIBERTI, BUONACCORSO
16 Drawing of the swivel crane used in building the dome of Florence cathedral (Zibaldone 105 r.) 20.
GHIBERTI, LORENZO (1378-1455)
17 *Sacrifice of Isaac*, bronze panel for door of Florence Baptistry, 1401 (Bargello Museum, Florence) 10.
GHIRLANDAIO (byname of Domenico Bigordi) (1449-1494)
18 *Last Supper*, 1480 (church of Ognissanti, Florence) 43.
GIOTTO (c.1267-1337)
19 *St Francis expelling the devils from Arezzo*, 1297-99 (upper church of St Francis, Assisi) 12.
GOZZOLI, BENOZZO (1420-1497)
20 *Procession of the Magi*, 1459. Detail, with portraits of members of the Medici family (Chapel of the Palazzo Medici-Riccardi, Florence) 28.
INGRES, DOMINIQUE (1780-1867)
21 *Death of Leonardo*, 1818 (Musée du Petit Palais, Paris) 60.
LEONARDO
– Paintings
22 *Adoration of the Magi*, 1481-82 (Uffizi Gallery, Florence) 26-27; **23** *Annunciation*, 1472-75 (Uffizi Gallery, Florence) 18-19; **24** *Annunciation* for Pistoia Cathedral, c.1478 (Louvre, Paris) 18; **25** *Bacchus*, 1515 (Louvre, Paris) 51; **26** *La Belle Ferronnière*, 1490-95 (Louvre, Paris) 39; **27** *Benois Madonna*, c.1478 (Hermitage Museum, St Petersburg) 38; **28** *Last Supper*, 1495-97 (Santa Maria delle Grazie, Milan) 42-45; **29** *Mona Lisa*, c.1503-1505 (Louvre, Paris) 38, 50-51; **30** *Madonna with the Carnation*, 1480 (Alte Pinakothek, Munich) 51; **31** *The Musician*, c.1490 (Pinacoteca Ambrosiana, Milan) 39; **32** *Portrait of Cecilia Gallerani (Lady with an Ermine)*, 1488 (Czartoryski Museum, Cracow) 39; **33** *Portrait of Ginevra de' Benci*, 1474 (National Gallery of Art, Washington, D.C.) 38; **34** *Portrait of Isabella d'Este*, 1500 (Louvre, Paris) 39; **35** *St John the Baptist*, 1513-16 (Louvre, Paris) 61; **36** *The Virgin and Child with St Anne*, 1510-13 (Louvre, Paris) 54-55; **37** *The Virgin of the Rocks*, 1483-86 (Louvre, Paris) 32-33; **38** *The Virgin of the Rocks*, 1503-06 (National Gallery, London) 32.
– Drawings and studies
39 Cartoon for *The Virgin and Child with St Anne*, 1498 (National Gallery, London) 55; **40** Compositional study for *The Virgin and Child with St Anne* (Accademia Gallery, Venice) 54; **41** *The Deluge*, c.1516 (WC 12380) 50; **42** Drawings of costumes for the "festa del paradiso", 1490 (Royal Library, Windsor) 31; **43** Drawing of hanged man, connected with the execution of Bernardo Baroncelli, c.1479 (Musée Bonnat, Bayonne) 29; **44** Drawing of a plough, Leonardo's personal emblem (Royal Library, Windsor) 6; **45** Drawings of regular bodies for Luca Pacioli's *De divina proportione*, 1496-1503 (ML) 40; **46** Drawing of roof for Milan Cathedral, 1487-88 (AC 310 v-b.) 35; **47** Drawing of the swivel crane used in building the dome of Florence Cathedral (AC 965r.) 20; **48** *Female head* (Gabinetto dei disegni e delle stampe, Uffizi Gallery, Florence) 18; **49** *The Flood*, c.1516 (WC 12380) 50; **50** *Grotesque portrait*, c.1515 (Christ Church, Oxford, inv. 0033) 42; **51** *La Scapigliata (lady with hair undone)*, 1490 (Pinacoteca Nazionale, Parma) 39; **52** *Landscape of the Arno Valley*, 1473 (Gabinetto dei disegni e delle stampe, Uffizi Gallery, Florence) 7; **53** Map of Pisa and mouth of the Arno, c.1503 (MII 52 v., 543 r.) 53; **54** Perspective study for the *Adoration of the Magi*, c. 1481 (Gabinetto dei disegni e delle stampe, Uffizi Gallery, Florence) 27; **55** Plan for casting the Sforza monument (MII 157 r.) 31; **56** Plan for the Château de Remorantin, 1517-18 (ARC 269 r.) 61; **57** Plans for symmetrically designed churches (MB 17 v.) 35; **58** Preparatory drawing for *Adoration of the Magi*, c.1481 (ARC) 26 a.; **59** Preparatory drawing for *Adoration of the Magi*, c.1481 (Ecole des Beaux-Arts, Paris) 26 c.; **60** Preparatory drawing for the *Adoration of the Magi*, c.1481 (Fitzwilliam Museum, Cambridge, England) 26 b.; **61** Preparatory drawing for the drapery covering the knees of *The Virgin and Child with St Anne* (Royal Library, Windsor) 54; **62** Preparatory drawings for an equestrian monument, 1508-10 (WC 13356) 31; **63** Preparatory drawing with mountain ranges for *The Virgin and Child with St Anne*, 1498 (WC 12410) 50; **64** Preparatory drawing for *Portrait of Isabella d'Este* (Royal Library, Windsor) 38; **65** Preparatory drawing with storm over a valley for *The Virgin and Child with St Anne* (Royal Library, Windsor) 54; **66** Preparatory study for the *Last Supper*, c.1495 (WC 12542 r.) 42; **67** *Self-portrait*, 1512 (Biblioteca Reale, Turin) 61; **68** Study for angel in *The Virgin of the Rocks*, c.1483 (Biblioteca Reale, Turin) 38; **69** Study of angel's head for *The Virgin of the Rocks*, c.1483 (Royal Library, Windsor) 32; **70** Study of the arm, c.1512 (Royal Library, Windsor) 37; **71** Study for armoured vehicle (British Museum, London) 47; **72** Study for ball and roller bearings (MI 101 v.) 59; **73** Studies of bird flight (BFC 7 v.; 8 r.) 56; **74** Studies of the cardiac muscle, c.1512 (Royal Library, Windsor) 36; **75** Study for chains (MI 10 r.) 59; **76** Study for cogged wheels (MI 5 r.) 59; **77** Study for coupling (MI 62 r.) 59; **78** Studies of the cranium, c.1512 (Royal Library, Windsor) 36; **79** Study of drapery, c.1478 (Louvre, Paris) 15; **80** Study of escapement (MI 12 r.) 59; **81** Study for excavating machine (AC 1 v.b.) 52; **82** Study for figure of St James in the *Last Supper*, c. 1495 (WC 12552) 42; **83** Study for flying machine (AC 276 r.b.) 56; **84** Study of flying machine with partially fixed wing (AC 309 v.a.) 56; **85** Studies of foetuses, c.1512 (Royal Library, Windsor) 37; **86** Study for foundry (WC 12647) 46; **87** Studies of heads for *The Battle of Anghiari*, c.1504 (Szépnuïveszeti Museum, Budapest) 49; **88** Study of horseman with lance, c.1483 (WC 12653) 46; **89** Study of horses and riders for the *Battle of Anghiari*, c. 1504 (Louvre, Paris) 49; **90** Study for lock gate (AC 240 r.c.) 52; **91** Study for machine gun (AC 56 v.) 47; **92** Study of machine for converting alternating to continuous motion (AC 30 v.) 58-59; **93** Study for mortar (AC 9 v. top) 46; **94** Study for parachute (AC 381 v.a.) 56; **95** Study for perspectograph (AC 1 b r.a.) 13; **96** Study of plants for *The Virgin of the Rocks*, c. 1483 (Royal Library, Windsor) 32; **97** Study for propeller (MB 83 v.) 56; **98** Study for pulley (MI 87 r.) 59; **99** Study of rearing horse, c.1490 (WC 123582) 24; **100** Study of rocks and aquatic birds for *The Virgin of the Rocks*, c.1483 (Royal Library, Windsor) 32; **101** Study for screw (MI 58 r.) 59; **102** Study for Serravalle tunnel (MI11 r.) 53; **103** Study of the thorax, c.1512 (Royal Library, Windsor) 37; **104** Study of towers (MII 93 v.) 47; **105** Study for a wing (AC 22 v. b.) 57; **106** Study for articulated wing (AC 308 r.a.) 57; **107** Studies for a wing with apertures (AC 74 r.; 309 v.b.) 56; **108** Study for integrated wing (AC 313 r.a.) 57; **109** Study for worm gear (MI 17 v.) 59; **110** Vitruvian man, c.1492 (Accademia Gallery, Venice) 36.
– Works attributed to Leonardo
111 *Lady with pearls*, now thought to be a work of the Bolognese school (Pinacoteca Ambrosiana, Milan) 39.
LIPPI, FILIPPO (c.1406-1469)
112 *Annunciation*, 1437-40 (church of San Lorenzo, Florence) 19.
LIPPI, FILIPPINO (1457-1537)
113 *Adoration of the Magi*, 1496 (Uffizi Gallery, Florence) 27.
LORENZO DI CREDI (1459-1537)
114 *Portrait of old man* recognized as Perugino, c.1490 (Gabinetto dei disegni e delle stampe, Uffizi Gallery, Florence, inv. 237E) 15.
MARTINI, FRANCESCO DI GIORGIO (1439-1502)
115 Page from *Treatise on military and civil architecture* (Biblioteca Laurenziana, Florence) 30; **116** Page from *Treatise on military and civil architecture* with lifting machine (Biblioteca Laurenziana, Florence) 58.
MASACCIO (byname of Tommaso di ser Giovanni di Mone Cassai) (1401-1428)
117 *Adoration of the Magi*, 1426 (Staatliche Museen, Berlin) 26; **118** *The Tribute Money*, 1427-28 (Brancacci Chapel, church of Santa Maria del Carmine, Florence) 11; **119** *The Trinity*, 1427 (church of Santa Maria Novella) 12.
MASOLINO DI PANICALE (c.1383-1440) AND MASACCIO
120 *The Virgin and Child with St Anne*, 1420 (Uffizi Gallery, Florence) 55.
NANNI DI BANCO (1380/90-1421)
121 *Four Crowned Saints*, 1412-16 (Orsanmichele, Florence) 10.
PAOLO UCCELLO (byname of Paolo di Dono) (1397-1475)
122 *The Battle of San Romano*, 1456-1460 (Uffizi Gallery, Florence) 10.
PIERO DELLA FRANCESCA (1415/20-1492)
123 *Annunciation* (Galleria Nazionale dell'Umbria, Perugia) 12; **124** *Baptism of Christ*, c.1448-50 (National Gallery, London) 13.
RAPHAEL (Raffaello Sanzio) (1483-1520)
125 *The School of Athens*, c.1508 (Stanza della Segnatura, Vatican) 61; **126** Preparatory drawing for *The Dispute over the Sacrament* with portrait of Bramante, 1509 (Vatican Museum, Rome) 34.
RUBENS, PETER PAUL
127 Copy of the central section of *The Battle of Anghiari* (Louvre, Paris) 49.
UTILI, GIOVANNI BATTISTA (1465/70-1516)
128 *Three Archangels with Tobias*, 1470. Detail showing the construction site of Santa Maria del Fiore (Bartolini and Salimbeni collection, Florence) 21.
VAN DER GOES, HUGO (1435/40-1482)
129 *Adoration of the Shepherds*, 1476-78, detail (Uffizi Gallery, Florence) 11.
VAN EYCK, JAN (c.1390-1441)
130 *Giovanni Arnolfini and his wife*, 1434 (National Gallery, London) 11.
VERROCCHIO (byname of Andrea di Francesco di Cione) (1435-1488)
131 *David*, c.1465 (Bargello Museum, Florence) 22; **132** *Doubting Thomas*, c.1483 (Orsanmichele, Florence) 22; **133** *Equestrian Monument to Bartolomeo Colleoni*, 1497-88 (Campo dei Santi Giovanni e Paolo, Venice) 24, 31; **134** *Winged putto*, 1475-80 (courtyard of Palazzo Vecchio, Florence) 22; **135** *Study of male nude*, c.1470 (Gabinetto dei disegni e delle stampe, Uffizi Gallery, Florence) 14.
VERROCCHIO AND LEONARDO
136 *Baptism of Christ*, 1472-75 (Uffizi Gallery, Florence) 16-17; **137** Study for head of Venus. Sketch for *Venus and Cupid*, c.1475 (Gabinetto dei disegni e delle stampe, Uffizi Gallery, Florence) 15.
VIGONNISE BARB
138 *Portrait of Luca Pacioli* (Capodimonte Museum, Naples) 40.

◆ INDEX

◆ CREDITS

The original and previously unpublished illustrations in this book may only be reproduced with the prior permission of Donati-Giudici Associati, who hold the copyright.

The illustrations are by: Giovanni Bernardi (pp.8-9), Simone Boni (pp.20-21), L.R. Galante (pp.40-41, 46-47), Roberto Lari (pp.30-31), Andrea Ricciardi (pp.6-7, 28-29, 34-35, 52-53), Sergio (cover, pp.4-5, 12-13, 14-15, 16-17, 22-23, 24-25, 36-37, 44-45, 48-49, 56-57, 60-61).

All efforts have been made to trace the copyright-holders of the other illustrations in the book. If any omissions have been made, this will be corrected at reprint.

Thanks are due to the following institutions and individuals for their permission to reproduce photographs: Alte Pinakothek, Munich; Biblioteca Reale, Turin; Collezione Bartolini e Salimbeni, Florence; Czartoryski Museum, Cracow; Fitzwilliam Museum, Cambridge, England; Galleria degli Uffizi, Florence; Galleria Nazionale dell'Umbria, Perugia; Hermitage Museum, St Petersburg; Louis F. Hyde Collection, Glen Falls, New York; Musée Bonnat, Bayonne; Musée du Louvre, Paris; Musei Vaticani, Rome; Museo Civico Correr, Venice; Museo di Capodimonte, Naples; Museo Nazionale del Bargello, Florence; National Gallery, London; National Gallery of Art, Washington, D.C.; Pinacoteca Ambrosiana, Milan; Pinacoteca Nazionale, Parma; Staatliche Museen, Berlin;

PHOTO SCALA/FLORENCE: 2, 4, 5, 7, 9, 15, 17, 18, 20, 22, 23, 26, 27, 28, 29, 30, 31, 32, 34, 35, 36, 67, 112, 113, 119, 120, 121, 122, 123, 125, 129, 131, 135, 136.
MARCO QUATTRONE: 19

Thanks are due to the Istituto di Scienza delle Costruzioni of the Faculty of Architecture, University of Florence, for granting permission to publish the models of Leonardo's machines reproduced on page 20.